Passion for Another World

Giving Witness of the Hope That Is in Us

WCC Internal Encounter of Churches,
Agencies and Other Partners on the World Bank and the
International Monetary Fund

Geneva, 11-12 September 2003

edited by Rogate R. Mshana

This document comprises the papers delivered at a meeting called by the World Council of Churches to discuss the policies of the World Bank and International Monetary Fund, held in September 2003 in Geneva.

Contents

Introduction

A COMMON ECUMENICAL UNDERSTANDING OF IFI POLICIES

Rogate R. Mshana

Background

Since its inception, the World Council of Churches has been committed to issues of economic justice. God's option for the poor was the basic theological paradigm for this work. A process called Economy as a Matter of Faith was initiated by the WCC in 1992 to underline that faith is at the heart of struggles for economic justice.

Over the years, a wide spectrum of economic justice issues has been covered by the WCC's Justice, Peace and Creation Team, raising critical questions about the global economic and financial system. Some of the major discussions in the WCC have been about transnational corporations and human development, decent work, employment and unemployment, the international financial system, and more recently the development of alternatives to economic globalization, focusing on a just finance system, just trade and an alternative to the neoliberal economic paradigm.

The ecumenical movement has always focused on the ethically unacceptable consequences of decisions made by the Bretton Woods institutions. The challenge for the WCC and the ecumenical movement has been to take a more proactive role and – together with the churches – to reflect in more detail on the problems that they have identified in the policies of international financial institutions (IFIs) and to seek alternatives. The commitment of the ecumenical movement is based on the conviction that there is no policy that cannot be changed; no economic system that cannot be reformed if it does not serve the interests of the poor and instead accumulates wealth at the expense of the poor and of God's creation.

The WCC General Assembly at Harare (1998) gave clear directions for future work on economic justice:

> Work on globalization should build upon and strengthen existing initiatives of churches, ecumenical groups and social movements, support their cooperation, encourage them to take action, and form alliances with other partners in civil society working on issues pertinent to globalization, particularly formulating alternative responses to the activities of transnational corporations, the Organization for Economic Cooperation and Development, the International Monetary Fund, the World Bank, the World Trade Organization, the International Labour Office and related multilateral agreements, in order to identify the harmful as well as positive impact of their policies in a competent manner.

In January 2001 the WCC Central Committee translated this commitment into a policy with these recommendations:

1   The member churches and the WCC develop a comprehensive ecumenical theological analysis of economic globalization and its impact on the churches, and provide a theological basis for the search for alternatives, coordinated by the Cluster on Issues and Themes. This work should include study, sharing of information, and training workshops. The Central Committee encourages continued cooperation with ecumenical partners in this area, for example with the World Alliance of Reformed Churches' work on economic justice.

2   The WCC strengthen its capacity by involving representatives of churches affected by economic globalization, ecumenical organizations, social movements, research institutions and people with political and economic expertise in this area and maintain constant contacts. The WCC must contribute to the developing global response to the challenges of economic globalization that is rooted in local initiatives, so that its representatives can engage effectively at the global level. This work includes among other things: (a) the development of guidelines for churches aiming at a consistent response from member churches and ecumenical organizations to institutions promoting economic globalization; (b) the sharing of information in order to raise awareness of the adverse affects of economic globalization.

3   The WCC focus on searching for alternatives to economic globalization based on Christian values in the following three areas: (a) The transformation of the current global market economy to embrace equity and values that reflect the teachings and example of Christ; (b) Development of just trade; (c) Promotion of a just financial system, free of debt bondage, corrupt practices and excessive speculative profit making.

The WCC has worked closely with WARC, the LWF, CEC and theologians to develop the theological basis for challenging economic globalization through a series of regional church consultations. Among the subjects of such consultations were the WCC/WARC consultation on globalization (1999); the impact of globalization in Central and Eastern Europe (2001); the impact of globalization in the Pacific (2001); economy in the service of life (2002); globalizing the fullness of life (2003); and accompanying the consultation by churches in North America, focusing on Trade (NAFIA) (2004).

The WCC responded positively to an invitation from the World Bank and the IMF to enter into dialogue. A staff delegation from the IMF visited the WCC in July 2000, requesting further dialogue. Additionally, there was an invitation to the WCC General Secretary to attend the World Bank/Civil Society Joint Facilitation Committee meeting in Washington, DC (December, 2001). A joint letter of 17 September 2002 was also received by the General Secretary from the President of the World Bank and the Managing Director of the IMF.

The WCC has embarked on a process of encounters with IFIs so as to create the space for churches and other ecumenical partners to raise their critical concerns. Based on the testimonies and research findings of many in the WCC network, it is abundantly clear that the excluded and poor people of the world are in fact adversely affected by the economic policies of the IFIs. The commodification of public goods (such as the privatization of water) at the behest of the World Bank and IMF, for example, causes desperate hardship for the poor in many countries in the southern hemisphere. This only underlines the need for dialogue with the IFIs about their philosophy and programme methodologies for the alleviation of poverty.

It is the WCC's understanding that the eradication of poverty cannot be achieved through the austerity policies of the IFIs. The background document Lead Us Not Into Temptation: Churches' Response to the Policies of International Financial Institutions was prepared by a group of experts to guide this critique of the IFIs. The document was sent to churches by the WCC General Secretary and was also shared with a wide range of social movements. The President of the World Bank and the Managing Director of the IMF and some staff of these institutions also received copies of the document. It has formed the basis for the WCC's encounters with the World Bank and IMF.

The first external encounter between the WCC and the IFIs was held in February 2003 in Geneva and focused on institutional formation, the mandates and perspectives of these institutions, wealth creation and social justice, and the commodification of public goods. A second encounter took place in October 2003 in Washington, DC. The report for the first encounter is called 'Wealth Creation and Justice'. At the same time, several other church groups and related agencies have also entered into discussions with the IFIs. In order to sharpen understandings of the policies of IFIs, and to develop a more coordinated and coherent ecumenical response, the WCC called for an internal encounter for the exchange of experiences: specifically, how the ecumenical movement can respond effectively to the policies of IFIs.

INTERNAL ENCOUNTER OBJECTIVES
- To elaborate a common vision and coherent strategies within the ecumenical movement to address the policies implemented by IFIs.
- To enable representatives from churches, agencies and social movements to search for consistent and effective ways to promote ecumenical responses to the policies of the World Bank and IMF from the perspective of people in poverty and the marginalized.
- To discuss the issues which have to be raised with the World Bank and IMF at the second external encounter.

Main questions raised
- What are the critical questions that churches and ecumenical bodies should raise in response to the policies of the World Bank and IMF (poverty reduction policies, debt, liberalization, privatization and commodification of public goods)?
- Why should the ecumenical movement take a stand from the perspective of the spiritual, ethical and moral imperatives that need to be raised regarding the policies of these institutions?
- How should the ecumenical movement develop strategies for resistance and offering alternatives?

- What are the expectations from the second encounter between the WCC, the World Bank and the IMF and what could be the long-term challenges in this process?

This book contains the various papers discussed during this encounter, together with conclusions. There is still a marked difference between the presentations of the IFIs and those of the World Council of Churches. Dr. Raiser's paper (chapter 3) was the theological framework for the discussions that followed. In addition, Bible study and worship inspired the whole encounter.

Rogate R. Mshana
Programme Executive, Economic Justice
World Council of Churches

April 2004

1

Commencement

Bob Goudzwaard

We live in a violent, rapidly changing world, full of risks and unexpected turns of history. We need to actualize our thoughts again and again in the light of some-times-bitter experiences.

For the first time in history, churches and ecumenical agencies from all over the world have met to discuss the policies and related activities of the international financial institutions. Such a meeting can only be fruitful if we are willing to be open and share in a truly ecumenical way – not only our own recent experiences, or our complaints, or our frustrations, or even our rationalized outspoken anger, but also our hopes, ideas and creative thoughts about the role of international agencies.

The ecumenical movement needs to inhale, to take breath in. The World Council of Churches, the Word Bank and the IMF have begun a limited process of encounters, designed to enlighten ourselves about each other and to sort out where we possibly can agree (or at least come to a better understanding) and where we clearly disagree. We met to compare our mandates and our ideas and concepts of development, and then jumped directly into a controversy about the privatization of water. We realized that we needed to dig deeper. Therefore, we took the joint decision to look at the necessary role of the state, to ask what real participation of the poor implies, and to discuss the need for democratic and representative governance, in a globalizing world in general and in the international institutions in particular. These issues therefore became the main themes for the next encounter. That encounter should be informed by your experiences, frustrations, dreams and hopes, and with the pains of the poor and the needy. If not, the next encounter will merely be a kind of elitist cycling in the air, removed from the hopes and despair of the smallest of God's people.

There is also the need to exhale, to breathe out, together. For let's be very clear: for most of us, such encounters are not self-evidently useful. After all, the increasing urgency of the problems of our time is already manifest in deepening social and economic injustice; in the progress of hard neoliberal convictions in the international arena; in the ongoing devastation of our global natural heritage, legitimized and rationalized (among others by President Bush) by the priority given to rich countries in their fervour for unlimited industrialization. These things are so utterly ruinous that we are called, by our Maker as much by ourselves, to wake up, to respond. For it has always been the conviction of the ecumenical movement that there is no policy that cannot be changed; that there is no economic system that cannot be reformed if it does not serve the interests of the poor.

Therefore, together, we have to search for alternatives, and begin to elaborate a common and coherent vision of hope, change and resistance. This will take lots of time, of course, but we should at least try to build a common ecumenical basis.

This breathing in and breathing out is our own internal ecumenical process.

However, to remain as open as possible, and to prevent possible misinterpretations of the policies of the IFIs, we also welcome wholeheartedly Katherine Marshall from the World Bank and Flemming Larsen from the IMF.

Let us look forward to a creative and truly ecumenical view of the role of the WCC, the IMF and the World Bank.

2

Past, Present and Future

Samuel Kobia

The World Council of Churches (WCC) has a long legacy of engagement on justice issues and economic justice in particular. The WCC, its member churches and the ecumenical family have addressed themselves to the issue of economic justice and sharing of resources in all parts of the world. Each and every WCC Assembly raises these issues.

In 1948, at its inaugural Assembly in Amsterdam, the WCC stated that justice was a desideratum in assessing both political and economic life. This marked the beginning of the legacy. In 1954 the Evanston Assembly viewed the doctrine of the responsible society as a basic tenet: the economic order could be just only if those people affected by it have the right and power to influence and bring about change.

At the Nairobi Assembly in 1975, delegates described the free market system as having an intrinsic exploitative tendency which concentrated power in fewer and fewer hands. The Assembly also discussed structures of injustice and struggles for liberation. In 1968, in Uppsala, the work on economic justice led to the establishment of the Commission on the Churches' Participation in Development (CCPD). In the work of the CCPD the language and paradigms used included 'people's participation', 'preferential option for the poor', 'empowerment' and 'dignity in participation': 'Poverty, we are learning, is caused primarily by unjust structures that leave resources and the power to make decisions about the utilization of resources in the hands of a few, within nations and among nations. Unjust structures are often the consequence of misdirected goals and values.'

An Advisory Group on Economic Matters was formed to further advance this ecumenical economic approach under the WCC CCPD. Several documents in the Ecumenical Approach to Economics series were published, including *Ecumenism and a New World Order: The Failure of the 1970s and the Challenges of the 1980s* (ed. Marcos Aruda, 1980) and *Transnational Corporations, Technology and Human Development* (ed. Marcos Aruda, 1984).

In 1983, at the Vancouver Assembly, the Justice, Peace and Integrity of Creation (JPIC) conciliar process began with an emphasis on the integrity of creation. The focus moved from an anthropocentric to a cosmic view, taking in the whole household of God – oikos. Many discussions also took place around the issues of socio-economic and ecological sustainability.

In Canberra in 1991 the Assembly noted the acquisitive materialism that had developed into the dominant ideology of the day. Delegates described the need for 'a new concept of value, based not on money and exchange, but rather on sustainability and use'.

In 1998 at the Harare Assembly, discussions centred on the vision and logic of globalization. The oikoumene is the unity of humankind and the whole inhabited earth. The logic of globalization was to be challenged by an alternative way of life

– one of community in diversity. This alternative was expressed as 'life with dignity in sustainable communities'.

At its meeting in Potsdam in January 2001, WCC Central Committee came up with a policy on economic globalization that emphasized the need to work for just trade and a just global financial system. The WCC is against the growing inequality, concentration of power and social exclusion caused by economic globalization. Its main goal is to promote life with dignity in just and sustainable communities.

In order to prepare for this ecumenical journey, several life-centred criteria are used to evaluate new social and institutional arrangements at all levels of decision making:

- Equity as basic fairness that also extends to other life forms.
- Accountability as the structuring of responsibility towards one another and the earth itself.
- Participation as the optimal inclusion of all involved.
- Sufficiency as a commitment to meet the basic needs of all life, and subsidiarity as determining the most appropriate level for decision making while supporting a downward distribution of power.

One might wonder why the WCC puts such a strong emphasis on justice. It is because justice is a gospel imperative. We have no choice but to get involved. Economics is very much a matter of faith, and as long as injustice exists we shall struggle to overcome it in all its forms.

At this point in its history the WCC is taking a qualitatively different approach. In the 1970s and 1980s it worked on confronting transnational corporations. There was no dialogue. Today, however, dialogue with the World Bank and the IMF provides a good framework and platform for engagement in order to reach mutual understanding. I place great value on this process and I am optimistic about positive outcomes.

3

Spirituality of Resistance

Konrad Raiser

WHY INTRODUCE SPIRITUALITY?
What does spirituality have to do with wealth creation, economic globalization or the commodification of public goods?

Of course, one would expect church people, especially theologians, to talk about spirituality and about values. They are the specialists in this area, while economists know best about the dynamics of the economic and financial system and how it actually works. As long as religious and spiritual leaders stay in their field of competence and talk about spirituality, the roles are clear. Spirituality refers to people's personal and most intimate convictions and motivations, whereas the economy follows objective laws that are reflected in mathematical formulas and models. The economy deals with the material side of human life, with the production and distribution of goods and services. Of course, people – at least some people – may also need spirituality and religion for their self-fulfilment, but providing for this need falls outside the realm of economics and is therefore usually neglected in the basic assumptions which enter economic analyses and calculations.

Why, then, should business people, bankers, politicians and representatives of international financial institutions (IFIs) seek dialogue with religious and spiritual leaders? Why should the President of the World Bank, together with the former Archbishop of Canterbury, initiate the World Faith Development Dialogue? Why should Professor Klaus Schwab, the President of the World Economic Forum, seek ways to form an advisory council of religious and spiritual leaders to accompany the efforts of the Forum?

These initiatives reflect a change in the understanding of religion and spirituality and their influence not only on people's private lives, but also in the public realm, including the economic and financial system. After four development decades, it is more and more obvious that dominant policies have been based on a one-sided understanding of how people act in society and have therefore not achieved their expected results. In many cultures, religion and spirituality continue to play a central role in shaping social interactions. The process of secularization, which has led to the privatization of religion in many Western societies, has not spread to other cultures in the same way as was expected. In fact, we are witnessing a resurgence of religion, not only as a spiritual, but also as a political force, not least in the context of responding to the impact of globalization.

What is more, we are increasingly aware that the functioning of the economy and the financial system presupposes and relies on a social fabric which is maintained through internalized values, attitudes and motivations, which in turn have their roots in religion and are regenerated through spirituality. This 'social capital' is reflected in virtues like trust, faithfulness, mutuality and solidarity, and has traditionally been taken for granted in economic analyses and thus not been accounted for. This is all the more surprising since the traditional language about economic and financial transactions is full of references to this foundation of social capital. Without 'trust', 'credit' and the readiness for 'sacrifice' and the expectation of 'redemption', no economy and no financial system would be able to function.

Today, we realize that the prevailing economic and financial policies that have been given global validity through the IFIs, have been using up and failing to replenish the social capital accumulated through generations and centuries. In fact, the values promoted by these policies reflect a reductionist view of the human condition in terms of homo oeconomicus and continue to undercut and erode the social fabric without which the economy itself gets caught in contradictions and dilemmas which it cannot solve with its own means. Thus, we see among economic and political leaders, including those responsible in the IFIs, an increasing interest in questions of social and religious values. The Global Ethic project of Hans Küng responds to this interest and finds broad support even among leading bankers.

This interest should be taken seriously, and many religious and spiritual leaders have responded readily, since they share the concern. However, important as religion and spirituality might be for regenerating lost social capital, they cannot simply produce it as the economy produces goods and services. Furthermore, they will fail if they avoid entering with their counterparts into a critical review of the very reductionist view of the human condition which underlies the prevailing economic paradigm. Even less must they allow themselves to be used to lend legitimacy to an economic and financial system which has failed to deliver according to its own criteria.

The Russian social philosopher Nikolai Berdiaev is often quoted as having said: 'My daily bread is a material problem. The daily bread of my neighbour is a spiritual problem.' In that sense, spirituality indeed belongs in this context. However, it will and indeed must challenge the prevailing logic of the economy, which assumes that following one's own self-interest is the most effective way of contributing to the well-being of all. Spirituality refers to that vital network of relationships within which all life, including human life, moves and is being sustained and which cannot be nurtured by satisfying material needs. Translating this understanding of the human condition into the language of the economy would mean placing the 'common good' above the satisfaction of individual self-interest and acknowledging cooperation and mutuality as decisive factors in interpreting and understanding economic life, instead of focusing on competition as the main driving force.

WHAT, THEN, DO WE TALK ABOUT?[1]

I have spoken in very general terms about 'spirituality' and 'religion' and assumed that spirituality refers to that source of energy which generates and regenerates a sense of purpose and recognition of values in social life and thus nurtures the social fabric. With these references I have followed a development in current public discourse, where spirituality has begun to attract renewed interest. In our increasingly pluralist societies, there is a growing interest in different forms and practices of spirituality, and we even observe the development of a market catering for the spiritual needs of people. Offering spiritual guidance can even become a new form of business, particularly among people whose material needs are more than satisfied.

On the other hand, we see a renewed quest for spirituality among those who are struggling for justice and human dignity; for them, spirituality refers to the energy which sustains people in the struggle. Experiences of defeat and prolonged oppression, but also occasional moments of victory and liberation, have led many of those engaged in people's movements to reappropriate the values of their spiritual traditions. It should be clear from these brief indications that spirituality has become a notion with relatively loose contours. For any responsible discourse it is necessary, therefore, to indicate what we are talking about.

Traditionally, 'spirituality' stands for a life of prayer and contemplation, for liturgy and the attitude of waiting upon God. In many traditions, spirituality has been associated with the disciplined life of monastic communities, which have consciously separated themselves from everyday life and its conflicting demands. For centuries, this ascetic tradition of spirituality, sustained by a life under the vows of poverty, chastity and obedience, has been upheld vicariously by those with a special vocation for prayer and contemplation. It was recognized that ordinary people could not submit themselves to those demands of a spiritual life except occasionally on retreats, pilgrimages and during the appointed periods of fasting.

However, the ecumenical movement has contributed to the rediscovery and reaffirmation of another dimension of spirituality which has always been alive in the church and not least among the monastic orders. From the early Benedictine motto ora et labora to the programmatic linkage between struggle and contemplation by the Taizé Community, from the missionary spirituality of the simple presence to the affirmation of a liturgy after the liturgy in Orthodox thought, there have been numerous attempts to live a life of spirituality in the midst of worldly struggles.

At the Nairobi Assembly of the WCC in 1975, the Moderator of the Central Committee, Dr. M. M. Thomas, pointed to this newly discovered dimension of spirituality with the phrase 'spirituality for combat'. He did not propose a spiritual upgrading of political struggles, nor was he interested in instrumentalizing spirituality as a moral preparation for combat. Rather, he wanted to point to the fact that the struggles for justice and human dignity have a spiritual dimension of their own. In fact, the powers that be, whether political, economic or financial, tend to cultivate their own spirituality, calling for sacrifices and asking for trust and faithful allegiance. The struggle for justice very often is a struggle about true and false spirituality, about true and false worship, or about serving God or an idol. M. M. Thomas added: 'Let us not forget that our struggle is not merely against others but also against ourselves, not against flesh and blood, but against the false spiritualities of the idolatry of race, nation and class and of the self-righteousness of ideals which reinforce collective structures of inhumanity and oppression.'

The impulse provided by M. M. Thomas to place reflection about spirituality into the context of worldly struggles has opened up a discussion which has found its echo in subsequent assemblies. Thus, following this line of thought, the

Vancouver Assembly affirmed: 'the spiritual struggle of the church must involve it in the struggle of the poor, the oppressed, the alienated and the exiled. The Spirit is among struggling people.' And the Assembly added the recommendation: 'That the churches explore forms through which Christian spirituality is manifested in the struggle for justice and human dignity.'[2]

In the period between the Assemblies at Vancouver (1983) and Canberra (1991) the search for 'a spirituality for our times' was the focus of intensive ecumenical dialogue and reflection. The report of Section IV of the Canberra Assembly under the title 'Holy Spirit – transform and sanctify us!' summarizes the affirmations on ecumenical spirituality arising from these dialogues in the following terms:

> Spirituality – in its manifold forms – is about receiving energy for life, being cleansed, inspired and set free, in every way being conformed to Christ. An ecumenical spirituality for our times should be incarnational, here and now, life-giving, rooted in the scriptures and nourished by prayer; it should be communitarian in celebrating, centred around the eucharist, expressed in service and witness, trusting and confident. It will inevitably lead to suffering; it is open to the wider oikoumene, joyful and hopeful. Its source and guide is the action of the Holy Spirit. It is lived and sought in community and for others. It is an ongoing process of formation and discipleship.[3]

The aspects of this description which are of particular significance for our reflection are the understanding of spirituality as energy for life; its incarnational character or rootedness in the here and now, in the world of human life and struggles; its orientation towards community and its openness to the wider oikoumene.

Gwen Cashmore and Joan Puls, animators of this ecumenical dialogue after the Vancouver Assembly, built their introduction to an ecumenical spirituality around the notions of openness, connectedness and earthedness.[4] Openness is the ability to transcend oneself, one's horizon; it is the willingness to make room for the other, to open oneself to the action of the Spirit; it is the manifestation of humility, the readiness not to insist on being right but to make oneself vulnerable and to be transformed in the encounter with others. Connectedness is the recognition that all life is sustained by bonds of community. All life participates in a delicate web of interconnections, in the flow of energy originating in God the Creator. Connectedness as a mark of spirituality finds its expression in the recognition and practice of cooperation, reciprocity and mutuality over a culture based on self-interest and competitiveness. Earthedness, finally, binds the ecumenical spirituality to the everyday conditions of life at a given time and place. Recognizing its finiteness and limitations, in constant dialogue with its culture and social environment, an earthed spirituality takes seriously the temptation to worship false gods; it accepts the task of 'discerning the Spirit' and nurtures the capacity for resistance, for endurance and staying power in the struggle to unmask the powers and principalities of this world (cf. Ephesians 6:10–13).

From an Asian perspective, Masao Takenaka has pointed to the way in which images and symbols rooted in the local culture can nurture the power of spiritual imagination and shape the human sense of responsibility. In an essay on Asian spirituality entitled *God is Rice*, he interprets a poem by the Korean Christian poet

Kim Chi Ha, "Heaven is Rice", which meditates on the highly symbolic character of rice as the daily food for people in Asia: 'The Chinese character for peace (wa) literally means harmony. It derives from two words: one is rice, and the other is mouth. It means that unless we share rice together with all people, we will not have peace. When every mouth in the whole inhabited world is filled with daily food, then we can have peace.' This leads to two important considerations:

> When we say that God is rice, we do not mean that we should worship rice. We take rice as the symbol of God's gift of life ... Second, if we acknowledge that God is rice, the symbolic source of the whole creation, and if we accept nature as our companion rather than as an object to be conquered or exploited, there will be a decisive change in our attitude towards the ecological issues.[5]

This approach to spirituality as rooted in the culture of people, especially the people of the 'Third World', is reflected also in the report of the 1992 Assembly of the Ecumenical Association of Third World Theologians in Nairobi. In his introduction, K. C. Abraham quotes the preparatory statement by the Theological Commission of EATWOT which, referring to the same poem by Kim Chi Ha, says:

> The cry of the Third World is a cry for life. It is a cry for freedom and dignity that constitute life as human. It is a cry for the rice and bread that sustains life as well as for the community that symbolizes and grows from rice and bread eaten in company ... Rice and bread for one person alone may not be spiritual because it may be selfish ... Or in the words of Nikolai Berdiaev, rice for myself alone may be unspiritual, but rice for my hungry sister and brother is spiritual. Thus our cry for life is a cry for the bread and the rice of life and for the spirituality of all the activities, processes and relationships bound up with producing and sharing rice and bread. Ours is a cry for a spirituality of and for life.[6]

The final statement of the Assembly, entitled 'A Cry for Life', refers especially to the cries of women, of black, indigenous and Hispanic peoples, as well as to the ecological movement. It states:

> We live our spirituality in creative response to the cry for life, the cry for God. We celebrate our spirituality in songs, rituals and symbols which show the energizing spirit, animating the community to move together in response to God ... There is no room for romanticizing spirituality. It is a cry for life, a power to resist death and the agents of death. Spirituality is the name we give to that which provides us with the strength to go on, for it is the assurance that God is in the struggle.[7]

And the statement describes this spirituality as a spirituality of commitment, rooted in a radical conversion to the God of liberation and life and able to inspire the search for alternatives beyond capitalism and socialism.

CAN SPIRITUALITY AND RESISTANCE GO TOGETHER?

It was the purpose of the preceding section to clarify the understanding of spirituality which motivates us and provides orientation in the encounter with those who carry responsibility in the present economic and financial system. The ecumenical discussion over these past 30 years of intense involvement in the development debate and in the struggles for justice and human dignity has led us to embrace a politically engaged spirituality which cannot simply be subsumed under the generalized notions of religious spiritual praxis, which comprises everything from Eastern forms of contemplation to modern programmes of spiritual self-realization. In particular, spirituality in this understanding transcends the individual and the closed horizon of the material conditions of life. It is the praxis of affirming and caring for life as a sacred gift from the Creator, which is being sustained only as it is being shared in community. By the same token, spirituality as the energy for life in all its fullness implies the commitment to resist all forces, powers and systems which reduce, deny or destroy life.

The background document *Lead Us Not Into Temptation*, prepared by the WCC to assist churches in their responses to the policies of international financial institutions, is guided by the same understanding of spirituality: 'There is … a long tradition of Christian spirituality which has been critical of the powers that be, even ecclesiastic. This tradition is based on loyalty to God above loyalty to institutions, ideologies and structures. This spirituality has given the powerless the strength and courage to oppose those that abuse power.'[8] It emphasizes that spirituality embraces all dimensions of life and is linked to the social, cultural, environmental and historical conditions of societies and their value systems. In this relational understanding of spirituality, God or the transcendent, the individual person, the human community and nature are intimately intertwined.

> This means that a spirituality that speaks only about the individual, or which believes the individual is the only basis for spirituality, must be questioned. All dimensions must be equally valued, as it is the case in so many social, cultural and religious traditions that value life in community higher than the dominant Western culture. Christians in various church traditions embrace a spirituality of life in community and of combating evil in confronting the powers of death. They stand against powers, be they economic, political, cultural or social, which deny to human beings, and the rest of creation, the possibilities of living a spiritual life. By extension, structures which break down the basic nature of fellowship of humankind and nature must also be named and opposed.[9]

A traditional understanding of spirituality would have questioned the very title of this presentation. From that perspective, spirituality and resistance stand for diametrically opposed forms of praxis. However, as the background document in its third section shows, the biblical tradition is full of evidence for a publicly engaged spirituality, including acts of non-violent resistance. In particular, the Hebrew prophets exemplify a praxis of spirituality which challenges unjust structures and unmasks the misuse of power. The same is true for the gospel accounts of the proclamation and action of Jesus. The story of the temptation of Jesus can be considered as a model of a spirituality of resistance. And the Apostle Paul frequently uses the imagery of struggle to describe the Christian spiritual life, a struggle not against flesh and blood and with weapons that cause harm or even death and destruction, but a struggle against 'the rulers, against the authorities, against the cosmic powers of this present darkness against the spiritual forces of evil in the heavenly places', fought with the weapons of truth, righteousness and faith to proclaim the gospel of peace (cf. Ephesians 6:10–17).

From this perspective, to speak of a 'spirituality of resistance' is not only entirely appropriate, it also makes us aware that the spiritual confrontation with all forms of power which refuse to acknowledge their accountability before God and the human community is inevitable. Spirituality stands for the active presence of the power of God in human life, which aims at enhancing life for all and defends those who are excluded: the poor, the strangers and those who have been declared outcasts. Therefore, spirituality will have to challenge prophetically any form of power which sets itself as absolute and is not legitimized by serving the common good. It will have to unmask false claims of authority and must seek ways of resisting policies and practices which serve to increase the power and wealth of the few while neglecting the basic needs and the right to life of the many.

Resistance can take many forms – from direct political intervention to symbolic actions, like prayer, fasting, public liturgies, boycotts, etc. Resistance as a form of spirituality does not follow the political logic which counts gains and losses and aims at effective change. Resistance is primarily a form of Christian witness, an affirmation of loyalty and obedience to God as the ultimate source of life over against all other claims of power and authority, whether political, economic, ethnic or cultural.

It is a spiritual resistance also against the absolute truth claims which exclude any alternative or dissent, as well as against the self-righteous dichotomies of good and evil. One of the hidden ways of exercising power over people's lives and minds has been the claim that after the collapse of the communist system there was no alternative to the prevailing economic paradigm, which was considered as reflecting the laws of nature. Any dissent was therefore treated as misguided, irrational or potentially dangerous and had to be suppressed. This tendency to absolutize a particular economic paradigm has had a paralyzing effect on political imagination and has contributed to a sense of fatalism, fear and defensiveness among people. Spirituality transcends the closed horizon of the system in hope and in love and thus becomes a resistance movement against fatalism, resignation and fear.

At the same time, a spirituality of resistance must guard itself against falling into the trap of self-righteousness by claiming absolute moral and spiritual authority and demonizing those who exercise power, ascribing to them evil intentions. The prophets and Jesus unmasked and condemned sinful structures, but Jesus welcomed sinners, offering them the newness of life in the kingdom of God.

M. M. Thomas speaks of the 'need to struggle for justice with an awareness of human solidarity in sin and acknowledgement of divine forgiveness'. Then:

> In moving from the concept of charity to that of justice we have to come to recognize the need for changing existing power structures. How can the struggles and conflicts to bring human dignity to the poor and the oppressed, even the power politics which oppose institutionalized violence with counter-violence, be kept within the spiritual framework of the ultimate power of the crucified Christ and the ultimate goal of reconciliation of all people in Christ?

Quoting José Miguez Bonino, he concludes:

> This requires recognition that 'our conflicts, even those which are most real and serious, can only be seen as penultimate. None of our battles is the final battle. None of our enemies facing us is the final enemy, the ultimate evil. Our contrasts are never black and white, always grey. Today's enemy must tomorrow be accepted at another level as a brother. Similarly, it prevents us from seeing our achievements in absolute terms.'[10]

SIGNPOSTS OF A SPIRITUALITY OF RESISTANCE

The spirituality of resistance is an act of witness in the midst of the power struggles of our world. It calls for constant vigilance in the effort of 'discerning the spirits'. Such spiritual discernment is needed in the dialogue with the representatives of the international financial institutions to be able to distinguish between the officially proclaimed goals and the operational values which come into play in responding to concrete situations. Discernment is equally needed concerning the allegedly irrefutable logic of the prevailing economic paradigm or the claims of rationality put forward by the proponents of 'political realism'. Václav Havel characterized this attitude of affirmative vigilance as 'living in the truth'. It is the courage to say 'no' and to say 'yes' which the message from the Amsterdam Assembly in 1948 described so powerfully.

The attempt to identify signposts for a spirituality of resistance leads us back to the conciliar process for justice, peace and the integrity of creation in which the ecumenical community has been engaged between the WCC Assemblies at Vancouver in 1983 and Canberra in 1991. The process culminated in the World Convocation on Justice, Peace and the Integrity of Creation at Seoul in March 1990. The most important legacies from this convocation are the Ten Affirmations on Justice, Peace and the Integrity of Creation. The affirmations are meant as a confession of faith in God, who promises life in wholeness and right relationships for all humanity. Each of the affirmations therefore begins with a statement which applies this faith in God's promise to specific situations of conflict around justice, peace and the integrity of creation. Where the traditional affirmations of faith were complemented by a rejection or condemnation of false beliefs and errors, the action-oriented affirmations of Seoul are being reinforced by the declaration 'we will resist', leading up to a final act of commitment.

The convocation concluded with a service of mutual commitment and covenanting for justice, peace and the integrity of creation. This service was built around the ten affirmations, which name explicitly the signposts for a spirituality of resistance. These include:

- We resist the exercise of authority that monopolizes power and prohibits transformation.
- We resist the forces that create and perpetuate poverty or accept it as inevitable or ineradicable.
- We resist the denial of rights to any racial, ethnic, caste or indigenous groups, and the exploitation of women and children.
- We resist the structures of patriarchy that perpetuate violence against women; which exclude their full participation in church and society.

- We resist policies that deny freedom of expression; that concentrate the communication power in the hands of a few.
- We resist doctrines of national security based on the use of weapons of mass destruction, military interventions and occupations.
- We resist the attitude to creation which treats it only as a resource for human exploitation.
- We resist all human greed that makes land a commodity, which denies the bonds between land and people, which devastates the earth for profit.
- We resist authority that abuses, violates or exploits children and young people.
- We resist all systems and structures that violate human rights; that tolerate torture, disappearances, extra-judicial executions and the death penalty.[11]

These signposts for a spirituality of resistance have not lost their validity in the 14 years since the Seoul Convocation. On the contrary, they continue to stand as a clear witness to an alternative system of values and offer specific criteria for the process of spiritual discernment. They do not prescribe any particular form of action, but they can serve to provide orientation for those engaging in dialogue about the policies of the international financial institutions.

Notes

1   I have drawn on two previous publications of mine: 'Life in the Spirit', in J. de Santa Ana, K. Raiser and U. Duchrow (eds.) (1990), *The Political Economy of the Holy Spirit*, Geneva, WCC, pp. 56–61; and 'Moral and spiritual formation', in K. Raiser (2002), *For a Culture of Life: Transforming Globalization and Violence*, Geneva, WCC, pp. 148–59.

2   D. Gill (ed.) (1983), *Gathered for Life*, Geneva, WCC, pp. 85, 89.

3   M. Kinnamon (ed.) (1991), *Signs of the Spirit*, Geneva, WCC, p. 112.

4   See G. Cashmore and J. Puls (1990), *Clearing the Way: En Route to an Ecumenical Spirituality*, Geneva, WCC.

5   M. Takenaka (1986), *God is Rice: Asian Culture and Christian Faith*, Geneva, WCC, pp. 18, 21.

6   See K. C. Abraham and B. Mbuy-Beya (eds.) (1994), *Spirituality of the Third World*, Maryknoll NY, Orbis, p. 3ff.

7   *Ibid.*, p. 197ff.

8   *Lead Us Not Into Temptation: Churches' Response to the Policies of International Financial Institutions* (2002), Geneva, WCC, p. 27.

9   *Ibid.*, p. 28.

10   Gill, *Gathered for Life*, p. 239ff.

11   *Now is the Time, Final Document and other Texts, World Convocation on Justice, Peace and the Integrity of Creation, Seoul 1990*, Geneva, WCC, p. 48ff.

4

Economics, Sustainable Development and Democracy

Peter Söderbaum

A MICROECONOMICS FOR DEVELOPMENT DIALOGUE

Having read the background document for this meeting, Lead Us Not Into Temptation, I am impressed and can only agree with many of the arguments. I share the opinions expressed about the seriousness of the social and environmental problems confronting us at various levels, from the individual through families, organizations, local communities, regions, nations and to the global level. Issues of poverty and injustice as well as environmental degradation in various parts of the world have to be dealt with in constructive ways through a dialogue with influential actors involved.

Churches in various parts of the world have an essential role in this. In Sweden I have to some extent followed how the archbishop and other representatives of the Church of Sweden increasingly participate in the development dialogue. A number of individuals as actors and collectivities make the judgement that present development trends will entail a number of problems. Active participation by the churches in this situation may well turn out to be decisive. Other actors, such as representatives of civil society organizations, academia, business, journalists and of course politicians, can contribute to a new vision.

I will focus here on the role of economics. International institutions such as the World Bank, the International Monetary Fund (IMF) and the World Trade Organization (WTO) all tend to refer to the conceptual framework and principles of neoclassical economics. While the IMF essentially is thought of in terms of macroeconomic policy, I will emphasize the microeconomic foundations of economics. Neoclassical macroeconomics is logically connected with neoclassical microeconomics. If one wishes to formulate a new macroeconomics then a new microeconomics is presumably the right place to start. It is furthermore argued that a more pluralistic economics will open the door for a constructive development dialogue.

Reference will be made to sustainable development (SD) as the main idea of welfare. SD has become institutionalized at the level of the UN, the European Union and in a number of countries, regions and local communities (through Local Agenda 21, for instance) and it represents a huge challenge for international institutions. If taken seriously, SD calls for a conceptual framework that differs considerably from that of neoclassical economics.

ECONOMICS, IDEOLOGY AND DEMOCRACY

Neoclassical economics is science in some sense, but at the same time ideology. As an example, assumptions about Economic Man are part of the neoclassical theoretical framework and these assumptions are specific in ideological and ethical terms. The specific version of institutional or ecological economics that will be advocated here is similarly specific in scientific as well as ideological terms.

'Ideology' is used in a rather broad sense as 'means–ends philosophy' more generally or in relation to particular spheres of activity. The concept of ideology thus includes (but is not limited to) established political ideologies such as liberalism or socialism. In addition, one can refer, for instance, to 'transportation ideologies', 'healthcare ideologies', 'poverty alleviation ideologies' and more generally 'development ideologies'. A transportation ideology may emphasize time saving, while more or less neglecting the environmental impacts of projects. Another transportation ideology may rely on the opposite priority, with environment as the first consideration. In connection with healthcare, centralization or decentralization of service is similarly an important ideological divide. Concerning poverty, economic growth through international competitiveness at the macro level, with expected positive trickle-down impacts on poor people, may be one ideological position, while emphasis on local self-sufficiency, local trade, appropriate technology and protection of local (regional) culture and environment may be another. It is assumed that each individual or actor as a Political Economic Person is guided by her 'ideological orientation'. An ideology or ideological orientation is often fragmentary and incomplete, but nevertheless suggests a direction of policy and behaviour.

These days, social scientists increasingly use the term 'ideology', but some scholars are reluctant and still refer to positivism as their theory of science. For this latter group, general statements based on objectivity and value neutrality are still the ideal. As I see it, something can be achieved within the scope of traditional ideas about science, but today, subjectivity in its different forms (hermeneutics, social constructivism, narrative analysis) is as respected among social scientists. Among well-known economists, Gunnar Myrdal regarded value neutrality as an illusion and argued at an early stage that 'values are always with us' in social science research (Myrdal, 1978). Myrdal saw himself as an institutional (rather than neoclassical) economist and wrote about development issues. He pointed to the 'fact' that values are involved in all stages of the research process. The scholar is faced with a number of choices. These include problem area, problem formulation, conceptual framework and theory, method, presentation of results, and much more. Such choices are based on values of some kind. Reference to established theory and method can of course be made, but in addition, subjectivity in the forms of values and ideology will enter the scene. Even decisions to rely on some specific 'established theory' are based on subjective values.

If it is admitted that economics is ideology and not only science, then a number of things will follow. For a long time, until about 1870, the discipline was referred to as 'political economics'. Today, it may be argued that it was a mistake to abandon this terminology. There are political and ideological elements in neoclassical economics and certainly also in alternatives to the mainstream, such as institutional economics.

This ideological or political element furthermore means that the imperatives of democracy also apply to science. Economics has to become pluralistic to better match the different ideological orientations in society. Instead of Kuhnian 'paradigm shifts', one has to think in terms of 'paradigm coexistence'. At any time, there may be a 'dominant paradigm', but advocates of this paradigm have to admit that the political bias of their theoretical perspective is a reason to accept the existence of competing paradigms and even encourage their development.

Economists connected with universities or international institutions such as the World Bank or the IMF will have to reconsider their 'expertness' and become much more modest. They have to learn about and recognize the existence of competing theoretical perspectives. They can no longer refer to neoclassical or some other economics as being the only 'correct' perspective. They are faced with a choice in ideological as well as scientific terms and cannot refer to theory as given and outside the scope of criticism. As an example, the World Bank and its representatives will be held accountable for the values that are part of their arguments and the same is true of university scholars like myself.

Citizens or representatives of political parties, churches, and environmental organizations should similarly feel free to debate the political and ideological aspect of competing conceptual frameworks and theories. While there will be criticism of a more scientific kind against a theory,[1] ideological criticism may be equally valid. In fact, the reasons why a person like myself advocates institutional and ecological economics are as much, if not more, ideological and moral than they are scientific.

In conclusion, it is argued that it is perfectly legitimate and indeed socially desirable to scrutinize and criticize a specific economic theory from an ethical or ideological point of view in addition to normal scientific criticism. In a society that claims to observe established imperatives of democracy this should be considered normal. The idea that science can be separated from politics has to be abandoned.

SUSTAINABLE DEVELOPMENT

While each citizen forms his or her specific ideological orientation, there is also a debate going on locally, nationally and globally about development ideas at a more collective level. A United Nations conference in Stockholm in 1972 pointed to environmental degradation in various forms as a key issue. Later UN conferences in Rio de Janeiro (1992) and Johannesburg (2002) added a social dimension of human rights, poverty alleviation and justice more generally to concern for the environment. Sustainable development has become legitimized – if not yet satisfactorily in practice, at least in the rhetoric – at levels from the global, through the European Union, Sweden as a nation, regions or counties, to municipalities and organizations. Since SD should also be relevant for the international institutions considered here, I will first discuss the meaning of SD and then whether neoclassical economics is at all compatible with it. If not, the World Bank and the IMF have to look in other directions for a constructive and useful theoretical frame of reference.

Sustainable development is generally understood in multidimensional terms. It is no longer enough to refer to GDP or income per capita. In addition, social and cultural dimensions, as well as dimensions referring to natural resources and the environment, have to be made visible as part of monitoring systems, decision making and follow-up systems. Non-monetary dimensions are not reducible to some alleged monetary equivalent.

SD is furthermore generally understood in ethical terms. This ethics refers to:

- relationships between individuals (groups) within a region;
- relationships between individuals (groups) living today and future generations living in the same region;
- relationships between individuals (groups) in a region and individuals (groups), present and future, living in other regions;
- relationships between human beings and other forms of life.

Actions undertaken in a region should not undermine living conditions elsewhere and in the future. Irreversible degradation of life-supporting systems should be avoided.

Social and environmental impacts are often uncertain. A 'precautionary principle' is therefore an important part of SD. The exact meaning of this term is not easy to define, but one part of it is that wishful thinking concerning impacts is not enough and that we can learn from a number of failures where the precautionary principle has not been observed (Harremoës, 2002).

Finally, democracy with its different imperatives is part of SD. Local Agenda 21 from the Rio conference builds on local mobilization of actors. While experts in some sense will still be needed, the idea is to counteract any tendency of experts to dominate completely the arenas where decisions are taken.

While sustainable development has become a catchphrase for many individuals and organizations, these actors may consciously or unconsciously interpret SD in different ways. Emphasizing environmental (rather than social) issues, I have elsewhere made a distinction between three different interpretations:

1. *Business as usual.* Here the tendency is to assume that the traditional mental map of neoclassical economics is still valid, with economic growth at the national level and profit maximization in business. SD is at best interpreted as sustainable economic growth in GDP terms.

2. *Ecological modernization.* According to this interpretation, it is recognized that there are important environmental and social problems that have to be dealt with and that a modification or 'modernization' of present paradigms, ideologies and institutions is needed. It is believed that minor adjustments, such as environmental management systems, environmental labelling and environmental impact assessment, will do the trick.

3. *Radical reconsideration of theory of science, paradigm, ideology and institutions.* While recognizing the importance of minor measures, as in (2) above, it is here regarded as wise to reconsider theory of science, paradigms, ideology and institutions as part of pluralistic dialogue. Something is already happening along these lines, but more is needed.

For some individuals and organizations, the business-as-usual interpretation may be dominant, or perhaps a combination of (1) and (2). The views or interpretations of other actors may belong to category (3), questioning the dominant trends of globalization and calling for some new thinking and action. There are often some (constructive or destructive) tensions between individuals within an organization with respect to interpretation of SD. The possibility of such heterogeneity among individuals should be kept in mind when approaching the World Bank, the IMF or the WTO. In attempting to characterize these institutions (the World Bank, for example), it should also be remembered that considerable differences may exist between the rhetoric of their specific documents and their practices. If the World Bank changes its rhetoric and indicates some new openings in relation to interpretation (3) above, for instance, this can be a significant beginning and step forward.

TOWARDS A RADICAL INTERPRETATION OF SUSTAINABLE DEVELOPMENT

A while ago I participated in a workshop initiated by the German government and held at the German Institute for Economic Research (DIW) in Berlin. One idea behind the workshop was that neoclassical economics is not enough in relation to present global and local problems of a social and environmental kind. There is a need for a 'sustainability economics'. I think this open-mindedness in relation to concepts and approaches is extremely important in the present situation. I will try to articulate a radical interpretation of SD a bit further and also consider its implications.

One first point is that a holistic approach is needed. It is not enough to focus on paradigms. The following four levels are identified as relevant:

- theory of science
- paradigm
- ideology
- institutions

A specific paradigm in the social sciences is normally connected with specific ideas and thought patterns related to a theory of science, ideology and institutions. If one wishes to open the doors to a different paradigm then one should at the same time suggest corresponding ideas, not only for the paradigm level, but also for the three other levels. The paradigm of neoclassical economics is very much dependent upon positivism as a theory of science. In terms of ideology, it emphasizes a specific idea of markets (that is, not very far from neoliberalism); specific kinds of institutions, related to trade in goods and services and other kinds of market exchange, follow from that.

Our institutional version of ecological economics differs from the neoclassical in all four respects, as will be shown below. A combination or 'package' of one theory of science, paradigm, ideology and institutions will be put up against another – one can hope for healthy competition between them as part of a pluralistic attitude.

Theory of science

Theory of science refers to the philosophy of acquiring knowledge. Positivism is the main philosophy in the natural sciences and also plays a role in economics and other social sciences. Positivism is mechanistic in perspective and characterized by an ambition to achieve objectivity and value neutrality. The idea is to look for causality and identify universal regularities or laws. Analysis is often reduced to a limited number of factors. Neoclassical economics, as an example, is to a large extent characterized by 'monetary reductionism'. Whenever possible, logically closed mathematical models are chosen and the idea is often to look for optimal solutions and to hand the results of analysis to decision makers.

Alternative principles for doing science – here connected with institutional economics – can be described as evolutionary, in the sense that history and path-dependence is important. Values are unavoidable and subjectivity is important. The approach is holistic rather than reductionist and the positivistic search for regularities is replaced largely by 'contextualism', where 'uniqueness' is as relevant as regularities and common features. In terms of method, case studies play an important role. Rather than equations, 'pattern models' that may be fragmentary are used to order activities and events in time. The issue of values in a society that claims to be democratic calls for approaches where interactive learning and dialogue are part of the problem-solving process. The idea is to illuminate an issue in relation to different ideological orientations, rather than to point out optimal solutions.

This alternative approach suggests that individuals as actors are important. Social science research can be carried out in the form of tape-recorded interviews with actors or stakeholders (influential or otherwise) related to an issue. How does actor A understand sustainable development and how does this understanding influence behaviour, activities, projects and policies at a more practical level? Studies of public debate in newspapers are equally relevant. Here again, hermeneutics and narrative analysis could be applied. The scholar participates in an interactive learning process with the many kinds of actors involved.

As an example, leading actors in the World Bank or the IMF may be approached in a dialogue about their understanding of SD and their attitudes to transnational business, etc. Representatives of NGOs, churches or universities can be approached in a similar manner. Actors at a local and regional level are of course as relevant to study as the more 'global' actors. Self-reflection and constructive ideas as part of problem-solving processes are among the possible results. In addition, various documents from these organizations can be scrutinized with respect to their content.

Paradigm

A paradigm stands for 'theoretical perspective' with a related conceptual framework. Neoclassical economics exemplifies a paradigm and is essentially positivistic with respect to theories of science. As is well known, it is a theory with consumers and firms as the main actors and with state regulation and intervention as a possibility. Markets for commodities and factors of production are at the heart of the analysis and are understood in terms of supply and demand.

Among alternative theoretical perspectives or paradigms, institutional economists emphasize the evolutionary aspects of economic processes and the role of institutions, social economists emphasize social relationships and ethics, and ecological economists point to the fact that the economy and its actors and markets are embedded in an ecosphere and that there are limits to the 'source' and 'sink' capacities of the environment (lithosphere, atmosphere and hydrosphere). One academic journal refers to interdisciplinary economics, another explicitly to environmental ethics.

I will suggest a conceptual framework that represents an opening for values other than those of neoclassical economics, such as a commitment to sustainable development;[2] that is largely compatible with the current language of development; and that focuses on the behaviour and responsibilities of individuals and organizations.

The 'paradigm' is relatively coherent, but does not represent a logically and mathematically closed theory, as is the claim of neoclassical economics. Our version of institutional ecological economics may be characterized as follows.

Political-Economic Person

As an alternative to neoclassical Economic Man assumptions, a Political-Economic Person (PEP) is proposed.[3] This person is regarded as a potentially responsible 'actor' in a socio-psychological sense. Our PEP is not limited to the role of consumer and other market-related activities: a person's roles as citizen, professional and parent are potentially relevant to economic analysis. In addition to such roles, there are many different kinds of relationships, motives and interests. In connecting the different roles, relationships and motives of a person, one may refer to their 'identity'; relationships may be brought together in 'networks' and a person's 'ideological orientation' is regarded as the main guiding principle.

Economics and efficiency

A holistic and multidimensional idea of economics is assumed. Impacts of different kinds are kept separate and described in terms of impact profiles, rather than aggregated in monetary or other one-dimensional terms. Efficiency and rationality become matters of ideological orientation and political agreements about the direction of change. The efficiency idea of CBA can be accepted or rejected by an actor, depending upon their ideological orientation. It is unrealistic to assume that there is a consensus in society about this particular idea of efficient resource allocation. The attractiveness of 'eco-efficiency' (in terms of material input–output relationships) for some actors has to do with the fact that it responds to a different ideological orientation from that of CBA.

Decision making

Rather than thinking primarily in terms of maximization or other optimization, it is assumed that the individual makes decisions or relates to her context by 'matching' her ideological orientation with the expected impact profiles of each alternative considered. Habitual behaviour can also be understood in terms of matching ideological orientation with expectations connected with familiar situations. Decision making and habitual behaviour become matters of 'pattern recognition' rather than optimization in mathematical terms, although the latter need not be excluded as a possibility. Aggregation in monetary terms is referred to as 'monetary reductionism' and is not regarded as fruitful if our ambition is to know what we are doing in non-monetary and ethical terms. Monetary impacts still play a role, but only as partial analysis.

Political–economic organization (PEO)

The only organization taken seriously in neoclassical theory is the profit-maximizing firm. Our interest refers to many kinds of organizations, where business companies represent a specific case. And even for business companies, the role of monetary performance in relation to various forms of non-monetary performance becomes an open issue. It is simply a matter of the 'business concept' or 'core values' of the company or, in current parlance, a matter of its ideological orientation.

There are many models of organizations. The stakeholder model is one, suggesting that it is not enough to think in terms of monetary profits and shareholder value. Other interested parties or stakeholders have to be considered, such as suppliers, customers, financing institutions, employees, and those living in the neighbourhood who, for instance, may be affected by pollution. While typically there are some common interests among the stakeholders related to an organization and within a specific category of stakeholders, there is also some heterogeneity. PEP is also part of PEO assumptions, in the sense that it is recognized that each individual as actor or stakeholder will have her particular ideological orientation. This means that the organization is regarded as 'polycentric'. Social change in an organization often depends on the entrepreneurship of specific individuals. If one organization implements an environmental management system, this is seldom the result of all individuals simultaneously becoming 'green' in their ideological orientation. Rather, it is the result of one or two individuals initiating a social change process that at some stage is broadened to include a large part of the organization.

Ideas about development and progress

Neoclassical economics, with its specific ideology, tends to legitimize a kind of 'consumerism' where more income and more commodities are assumed to imply a better life. Similarly, the assumption of profit maximization in business and the general emphasis on markets is highly ideological, with the belief that the 'market mechanism' will solve many kinds of problems and increase welfare in society (when encouraged through privatization, etc.). While a larger income may make life easier for people and monetary profits can have a positive role, our present challenge is to suggest a microeconomics that is useful in relation to sustainable development. As an example, it seems perfectly clear that SD can hardly be achieved at the macro level, if microeconomic units (individuals and organizations) pursue simplistic objectives in terms of more consumption and more profits. Impacts have to be considered in multidimensional terms and an open dialogue about ideological orientations appears necessary.

Market and non-market relationships

In neoclassical theory, markets are at the heart of the analysis, as exemplified by beliefs in the 'invisible hand'. Our starting point is instead that relationships between actors (individuals or organizations) are of a 'non-market' or 'market' kind. The idea that everything (or almost everything) should be interpreted in market terms is questioned. In organization theory, administrative and other kinds of relationships are considered relevant. And in the case of relationships between market actors, the supply and demand model of neoclassical theory is only one among many possibilities. There is often an important social component, for instance in business-to-business relationships. A supplier to ABB and ABB itself often have interests in common and should not exclusively be thought of as two independent firms with separate objectives. Each company is dependent on the other and often it is useful to think in terms of cooperation between companies in networks (Ford, 1990). One network of companies may in turn compete with other business networks. The relationship between two companies often includes more than one commodity; cooperative technological projects may be involved, etc. Furthermore, each social relationship between actors has a history, and trust is a factor in understanding changes in market relationships.

Cooperation is not necessarily a good thing in relation to SD. It may as well be negative, for instance when large business companies work together in cartels or when they lobby in Brussels and elsewhere to hinder the implementation of progressive environmental policy proposals.

Neoclassical market and international trade theory is simplistic in many ways. In table 4.1, I have tried to compare the neoclassical idea of markets with a view more in line with institutional theory. While neoclassical economics claims to point out the most efficient solution, the institutional approach as here indicated is more complex and open-ended with respect to ethics and ideology. Multifunctionality, for instance, has become an issue in international trade negotiations and this can be seen as a reaction to the simplistic neoclassical model of 'one commodity at a time'. Focusing exclusively on the monetary price of one commodity, such as wheat, while assuming that quality is equal and no other impacts are relevant, is a gross oversimplification. This oversimplification does not sit well with the multidimensional idea of sustainable development previously described. When carefully scrutinized, 1 ton of wheat from one supplier may differ considerably from 1 ton of wheat from another supplier, for instance in terms of toxic substances. And the farmer, while producing cereals of specific kinds, is also 'producing' an open landscape with specific aesthetic qualities at specific places. He is furthermore 'producing' employment for specific persons with specific family and community relationships. Some of us prefer 'ecological agriculture' to 'conventional agriculture' because we do not want pesticide residues in water. The conventional farmer is not only producing wheat, but also a whole array of 'products' that one may accept or prefer depending on one's ideological orientation. Such impacts are not limited to human beings, but include biotopes and ecosystems more generally.

To sum up, as an alternative to the mechanistic and generally positive neoclassical view, a conditional view of markets is suggested. The neoclassical reference to externalities may be part of this conditional view, but it is not enough. In principle, each market actor (and market transaction) can be scrutinized with respect to 'fairness' and judgements of fairness will differ depending upon ideological orientation. Among early institutional economists, John R. Commons referred to the fairness of prices, wages and labour relations more generally. Not unexpectedly, religious thinkers such as Thomas Aquinas pointed in a similar direction at a much earlier stage.

Table 4.1 The market as a phenomenon: two schemes of interpretation

	Neoclassical	*Institutional*
Time aspect	History not important	History important, path-dependence
View of the individual	Economic Man	Political–Economic Person (PEP)
View of the organization	Profit-maximizing firm	Political–Economic Organization (PEO)
Interaction between buyer and seller	Supply and demand	Multifaceted relationship between responsible actors
Goods and services	Homogeneity, one commodity at a time	Also heterogeneity, multiple transactions, multifunctionality
Motives for transactions	Profits or utility related to quantity and price (optimization)	Ideological consideration; 'monetary price and beyond' (matching)
Relations to other actors	Emphasis on personal gain for the firm (belief in the 'invisible hand')	Inclusive ('I and We paradigm', 'Person in Community')
Features of relationship	Independence: contract between parties with conflicting interests	Also cooperation; considerations of trust and fairness

Approaches to decision making

While many other components of neoclassical theory are useful for some purposes, cost-benefit analysis (CBA) as an approach to decision making is more questionable, since it is not compatible with normal ideas of democracy. The ideas of correct prices for purposes of aggregation at the societal level represent a specific ideology – why should this particular way of trading impacts against each other rule out all other ideological orientations? Ezra Mishan, himself a textbook writer on CBA (Mishan, 1971), argued that the use of CBA depends upon a consensus in society about a particular way of valuing one impact in relation to another. If there is no such consensus – and Mishan points especially to environmental issues of various kinds, where ideas about valuation vary considerably – then the CBA manual is no longer useful: it should be placed on a shelf to await a possible future consensus (Mishan, 1980).[4]

In the report by the World Commission on Dams (2000), it is argued that CBA should not be used to legitimize the building of large dams, especially in cases where resettlement of large numbers of inhabitants is part of the project. Issues of this kind are ethical – and simplistic mathematical operations are not very helpful in dealing with ethical issues. The WCD recommends a kind of multi-criteria analysis as an alternative. Positional analysis (PA) is another alternative that builds on Political–Economic Person assumptions and other elements of a different microeconomics, as indicated above (Söderbaum, 2000).

The purpose of PA is to illuminate an issue in a many-sided way with respect to:

- options or alternatives of choice;
- interests affected, conflicts between interests included;
- possible ideological orientations that are judged relevant by at least some of the actors or stakeholders.
- The main features of PA can be described as follows:
- Political–Economic Person assumptions
- Political–Economic Organization assumptions
- Imperatives of democracy
- Holistic conception of economics
- Conditional view of markets
- Systems thinking
- Positional thinking
- Analysis of activities and interests affected
- Rationality as an adaptive 'matching' process

While CBA is an aggregated, ideologically closed approach, PA is largely disaggregated and ideologically open-ended. Conclusions are conditional in relation to possibly relevant ideological orientations. Ideally, PA is carried out largely in cooperation with actors and stakeholders as a result of a well-documented stakeholder dialogue, but problems can also be approached in a more technical manner. However, listening to stakeholders at an early stage about their ideological orientation, their perception of the problem, and how different alternatives will affect them is a necessary part of any PA.

Ideology

As already defined, ideology stands for means–ends relationships in a broad sense and in a democratic society different ideologies are accepted and respected as long as they do not negate democracy itself. Ideology is not discussed much among economists and students of business.[5] This is unfortunate in many ways and may mean that important parts of problems are overlooked. If one is interested in sustainable development, then one has to discuss how SD as ideology relates to more established political ideologies, such as liberalism and social democracy.

Neoclassical economics, with connected ideology, has become accepted in many countries. Conservatives, liberals and social democrats alike seem to take for granted the mental map of neoclassical economics and thereby in large part the ideology that goes with it. Economic growth, for instance, is a common element in the ideology of many political parties. Focusing exclusively on GDP is certainly not compatible with SD, but the appropriate role of GDP in relation to non-monetary indicators of various kinds is still an open issue.

In recent years, neoliberalism has played an important role. According to David Korten (2001), neoclassical economics and neoliberalism, while different in some respects, are closely related. They share the same belief in the rationality and efficiency of the market in allocating resources and tend to connect welfare with GDP per capita. Transnational corporations can take over public services and privatization is regarded as beneficial to all. More profits and more consumption are generally assumed to be good for society. At issue, however, is whether one can speak about a 'society' at all, since individualism is at the heart of this approach. While neoliberalism is extreme in this sense, neoclassical economics also tends to legitimize the greediness of shareholders and consumers.

What is the alternative to neoliberal 'market fundamentalism'? Those who look for such an alternative will probably not get much help from neoclassical economics, except perhaps as a starting point in the search for a different ideology. Some other economics, such as the one indicated in this chapter, may be more helpful, as can many of the official documents that deal with sustainable development, poverty alleviation and similar issues. There are Green parties in many countries that are more or less established and there are NGOs of various kinds that contribute to the development dialogue locally, regionally and globally. Social protests that have taken place all over the world in connection with world summits and other similar arrangements (Seattle, Washington, Gothenburg, etc.) can play a constructive role, as can the arrangement of meeting places for those who do not share the politically dominant ideology.

Many are contributing to this broadening of the development dialogue. Churches can contribute. Since schools of business tend to avoid the more fundamental issues of ethics and ideology, others can step in to fill the vacuum. One example is the book Rethinking the Purpose of Business (Cortright and Naughton, 2002), to which thinkers from a Catholic social tradition have contributed. Among them, Charles M. A. Clark criticizes 'the free-market ideology' and refers to institutional economists like Thorstein Veblen and Gunnar Myrdal in a way not much different from ours.

My own ideological preferences are presumably similar to those of many others. First, I think that an ideology more in line with sustainable development should build on the primacy of democracy over market. Neoliberalism established the opposite priority and neoclassical economists are not much better when they apply their 'market glasses' to every possible issue. Our actor-oriented approach, with its PEP and PEO terminology, aims to re-establish the primacy of men and women as citizens and responsible actors. The individual is still important, but in a broader sense and not only in his or her market roles.

A second point is the primacy of social and environmental considerations over monetary and financial aspects. In all kinds of projects, programmes and policies, social and environmental impacts should systematically be made visible. Financial and monetary impacts are of course important, but the tendency to deal with economic efficiency exclusively in monetary terms (monetary reductionism) should be avoided.

Third, the agenda of neoliberalism is very close to the interests of transnational corporations. The idea seems to be to make it possible for transnational companies to penetrate every part of the globe. I suggest a priority for small and medium sized businesses (SME) with a more local and regional market as an alternative to the present dominance of transnational corporations. I am sceptical of the idea that every region should compete in terms of economic growth and with each other in marketplaces all over the world. There is of course a role for international business and for transfer of technology that represents good practice in relation to SD, but there is also a role for cultural and environmental 'protection', as will be further explained.

Institutions

Institutions can be seen as specific interpretations of the world and the manifestations of such interpretations. Neoclassical economics and ideologies close to neoclassical theory have supplied a number of models of the world that one may like or not like. These models have been more or less internalized by individuals in their different roles. In many cases, there are competing models or interpretations of a specific phenomenon and even competing institutions connected with such interpretations.

If models and interpretations play such an important role, then each individual can to some extent influence processes of institutional change. Let us take the example of the business company. Neoclassical economics suggests a model where a business company is an organization that maximizes profits in monetary terms. This particular interpretation is important in our society: the existence and responsibilities of a firm are closely associated with its monetary performance.

In recent years, environmental management systems have appeared as a different 'institution'. This model of a company emphasizes a specific kind of non-monetary performance: environmental performance. This model is furthermore manifested in professional terms through environmental controllers and certification organizations. Let us now assume that a specific company becomes certified according to ISO 14 001 (i.e. one of the environmental management systems). This change opens the door for a different interpretation of business companies that are certified. For them, not only monetary performance but also environmental performance counts. The result is a more complex model of the business company. If the number of individuals interpreting companies in this particular multidimensional way increases and the number of certified companies also increases, then this particular 'institution' is strengthened at the expense of other competing interpretations and institutions.

This is only one example of the ideological role of models and it is not difficult to understand how university education in economics tends to strengthen and weaken specific interpretations of the world. By referring to specific models of individuals, business companies, national governments, markets and the economy, not only universities but also the World Bank, the IMF and the World Trade Organization will either play a positive or negative role in social and institutional change processes, depending upon your ideological orientation. I have chosen to consult two documents in which the World Bank is involved (World Bank, 2001; DFID et al., 2001). In my judgement, the actors behind these documents have listened to some extent to the international debate involving international protest movements, etc. However, some remaining weaknesses can be identified:

- Although there is some move in the direction of interdisciplinary language, neoclassical economics still plays an important role. World Bank representatives have not abandoned the belief in cost-benefit analysis, as they repeatedly point to the need to further improve 'environmental valuation' in monetary terms, for instance.
- Not much is said about transnational business corporations, although they play a central role as part of development assistance. There seems to be a 'hidden agenda' not to disturb them, but rather prepare the way for their continued expansion. Page 9 of the DID report, for instance, argues '25 million agricultural workers may be poisoned each year'. If one is really bothered about these workers, such a statement should be followed by proposals for a World Bank policy to prohibit the export and use of many of the chemicals that cause these problems. The CEOs of the corporations producing these chemicals could be held responsible.

My conclusion from this somewhat superficial study is that in terms of rhetoric the World Bank is on the right path but something is still missing. In terms of the three possible interpretations of SD previously suggested, these World Bank documents fit into the 'ecological modernization' category. There is very little discussion about alternative premises in terms of theory of science, paradigm, ideology and institutions. It would have been interesting to carry out an actor-oriented study with leading individuals within the World Bank or other international institutions. This kind of dialogue would probably reveal some heterogeneity among staff members.[6]

DISCUSSION

Many of the people within the World Bank, the IMF and the WTO were educated as economists. Their understanding of economic theory and how it should be applied to international trade tends to define the arguments that are accepted or rejected at specific arenas. Markets are believed to do a good job when 'barriers of trade', such as tariffs and quotas, are removed. Competition is the path to progress in society and progress in a country is essentially seen as a matter of growth in GDP. 'Free trade' in some sense is good and 'protectionism' is bad.[7]

In the early 1960s I was teaching international economics at the department of economics in Uppsala University. Textbooks by Enke and Salera (1957) and Kindleberger (1958) pointed to the benefits of 'free trade' and warned against 'protectionism', the only possible exception being referred to as the 'infant industry argument' (implying that some industries can be protected for a limited time to learn about efficient low-cost production). But even this argument had its limitations, as the companies involved could become accustomed to a high level of protection and lobby for its continuation. What is good for the company may then be bad for society.

Since then, my early interest in international economics has been followed up every now and then. How do the writers of textbooks deal with 'protectionism'? And how do they deal with environmental issues? Is 'environment' a word that one can find in the subject index? How many pages are used to relate 'trade' and 'environment' (or 'natural resources') to each other? So far, I have always been disappointed when I examine these 600–800 page textbooks. My explanation or hypothesis is that there is something in neoclassical theory and ideology that closes the door to a number of issues that are judged important by an increasing number of politicians, professionals of various kinds and citizens. This theory – ideological as it is – does not appear to be compatible with present political dialogues in different arenas, whether local, regional or global.[8] Something new is needed. Rather than attempting to extend neoclassical theory, it seems as if a platform with a set of different basic assumptions about human beings, business companies, and efficiency, etc., has a better chance of being relevant.

In the one-commodity world of neoclassical theory, sellers and buyers look for the best possible price. If the price of a commodity such as wheat is low, this suggests that the suppliers have been efficient and that few trade barriers have affected trade. The low-cost supplier may be located in some region other than yours, and their sales may 'successfully' out-compete local suppliers in your region. The losers should then start producing other food products, where they may be more efficient and competitive regionally and internationally, it is argued. Or they should perhaps seek employment in other companies that are more successful in interregional and international markets. Another option is for workers to migrate to countries where production at the time is successful in terms of international competitiveness. Flexibility in this sense is regarded as a key to efficiency improvements and economic growth.

As discussed previously, this story is only a partial one and it is a matter of your ideological judgement whether these impacts and others (not being part of the story) represent progress in society or not. Employment at home is perhaps preferable to employment abroad. Long-distance transportation of food can be costly in environmental terms, even in cases where the monetary cost of transportation is relatively low. Reasoning of this kind has led to the 'multifunctionality' argument used by Norway, Switzerland and the EU in WTO negotiations. Not only the commodity traded is considered in multifunctional terms, but also the process of producing it, with all kinds of 'side impacts' on people, their culture/community and natural resources/environment. At issue, however, is whether the actors connected with the WTO will understand, since a large part of the international trade regime is based on neoclassical economics. Their ability to understand is limited by the education they have received.

Instead, a multi-layered idea of development – starting at the local and regional level – could be an option and would suggest a different kind of trade regulation. Small and medium-sized business is similarly encouraged and the present worship of growing transnational companies downplayed. Lately, we have seen an increasing number of failures of transnational corporations, even in one-dimensional monetary terms. Short-distance trade will reduce the environmental impact of transportation more often than not. It is, furthermore, a matter of one's ideological orientation whether 'protectionism' in a specific situation is legitimate or not. Personally, I see good reasons to protect the health of a population when it is threatened by the impacts of trade. Similarly, environmental protection is often justified, as we have learned since the Stockholm conference in 1972. A local, regional or national culture or community may need protection from commodities that may threaten this culture, and so on.

A World Trade Organization should not primarily protect the interests of big transnational corporations so that they can penetrate every part of the world, as is now the case. Competition is certainly needed in many places (for instance, at university departments of economics, where the neoclassical paradigm has systematically been protected), but competition can sometimes be destructive in relation to local and regional SD objectives of a non-monetary kind.

Institutions may change slowly and gradually as a result of competition between different ways of interpreting the world, as previously explained. However, at some stage in processes of social and institutional change, it is possible to inquire more systematically and deliberately into systems of international governance of the kind discussed. It is of course impossible to solve these problems immediately. But it is extremely important to rethink ideological priorities. While the interests connected with trade and transnational corporations have been considered more important than those related to health, culture and environment, this need not be the case in the future. Today, the impacts of such a ranking of interests are visible and some of us would like to see a different list of priorities.

It has been suggested that a World Environmental Organization could be instituted to defend environmental interests and counterbalance the activities of the WTO. I am sceptical about such an idea. As a thought experiment, let us instead think of a radical reconstruction of the WTO, so that it becomes a World Culture and Environmental Organization (WCEO) with the purpose of handling trade disputes. Trade should be seen as one among many means of achieving essential welfare objectives, such as those connected with culture, environment and health, rather than the present tendency to see trade and growth as more important than anything else. A change in denomination has of course to be followed up by a new philosophy and a new system of rules. New competencies are needed among staff members.

CONCLUSIONS FOR WCC STRATEGY

My conclusions have already been indicated. For the WCC, a continued dialogue with representatives of the World Bank, the IMF and the WTO is probably a good thing if one believes that actors within these organizations are really listening and learning. I believe that they have a lot to learn from people connected with different churches and the WCC as a cooperative entity. In addition, they would presumably benefit from the study of institutional and ecological economics and alternatives to the neoclassical paradigm more generally. However, not only those employed by the World Bank should be approached, but also the national governments as principals of the World Bank. This in turn points to the need for relationships with civil society organizations and more generally the need to participate in public debate.

As I see it, the ethics and ideology of neoclassical economics do not sit well with the ethics of churches and the WCC. I know that attempts have been made by the Vatican Council to improve dialogue with well-known neoclassical economists. Relationships of this kind are certainly of importance, but relationships with heterodox economists could be even more important in articulating a message from the WCC.[9]

Personally, I would like to see an increasing amount of people outside of academia who not only understand but also openly point to the ideological character of the dominant neoclassical economics and who ask for more pluralism at university departments of economics. Unfortunately, the present situation is one of monopoly for neoclassical economists, who simply deny the ideological features of their paradigm.

This brings us to our final point, which is not completely unrelated to biblical messages. In the kind of social change under discussion, it is easy to blame others and to forget about our own roles and responsibilities. I believe it is necessary to engage in debates where some are blamed and others praised. Criticism is a necessary part of public debate and democracy. However, it is extremely important to include your own category and person in such an attempt at critical evaluation. Thus, those of us who work from a university position can do a lot more to facilitate the transformation towards sustainable development. The role of university professors and universities has to be reconsidered. Hiding behind the dogmas of positivism and value neutrality is no longer a realistic option.

Notes

1   One of the latest examples is criticism by students of ways of teaching economics at universities in France. In the United Kingdom there is a web-based newsletter, Post-autistic Economics Review (www.paecon.net). A number of professors have participated in this newsletter and a book has recently been published (Fullbrook, 2003).

2   There is probably no single paradigm in economics that is good (or the best) for all purposes. In relation to present environmental and social problems, neoclassical theory may have something to offer by pointing to the 'polluter pays principle' and the idea of 'internalizing externalities', but other approaches may be even more powerful. PPP, as an example, will not be implemented until there is an ideological commitment among politicians and decision makers to take it seriously.

3   See Söderbaum (1998, 2000). Ideas of this kind have been discussed by European ecological economists such as Jakubowski (1999, 2000), Faber, Petersen and Schiller (2002) and Siebenhüner (2000, 2001).

4   It is of course possible that neoclassical economists can be successful in lobbying for CBA to be used as part of public policy and decision making in a specific area, such as transportation, or more generally. If as a result of such lobbying there are laws or other rules that CBA should be used, then the economists have been politically 'successful' in advocating for an economic growth (or 'net-value added') ideology rather than the SD ideology emphasized here.

5   There are exceptions, however, possibly suggesting a new trend. As an example, 'ideology' is emphasized in a book on business management and organization theory (Jackson and Carter, 2000).

6   For example, the first meeting in 1989 with the International Society for Ecological Economics (ISEE) was at the premises of the World Bank, Washington, DC. At the time, two leading members of the society, Herman Daly and Robert Goodland, were employed by the Bank.

7   It is a mistake to believe that scepticism about the neoclassical dogma of free trade is a new phenomenon. Even Charles Kindleberger's 1962 book pointed to a number of sceptics or persons who were less than enthusiastic about 'gains from foreign trade'. Gunnar Myrdal was mentioned.

8   Even a celebrated neoclassical economist such as Paul Krugman does not perform satisfactorily according to these criteria.

9   A person who knows more than others about the events, activities and journals of heterodox economists is Frederic Lee. E-mail: leefs@umkc.edu.

References

Cortright, S. A. and Michael J. Naughton (2002). Rethinking the Purpose of Business: Interdisciplinary Essays from the Catholic Social Tradition. Notre Dame, IN: University of Notre Dame Press.

Department for International Development (DFID), UK, Directorate General for Development, European Commission (EC), United Nations Development Programme (UNDP), The World Bank (2001). Linking Poverty Reduction and Environmental Management: Policy Challenges and Opportunities. A contribution to the World Summit on Sustainable Development Process (Consultation Draft). London: DFID.

Enke, Stephen and Virgil Salera (1957). International Economics, 3rd edn. London: Dennis Dobson.

Faber M., T. Petersen and J. Schiller (2002). Homo oeconomicus and homo politicus in ecological economics. Ecological Economics, Vol. 40, pp. 323–33.

Ford, David (ed.) (1990). Understanding Business Markets: Interaction, Relationships, Networks. London: Academic Press.

Fullbrook, Edward (ed.) (2003). The Crisis in Economics: The Post Autistic Economics Movement – The First 600 Days. London: Routledge.

Harremoës, Poul, et al. (eds) (2002). The Precautionary Principle in the 20th Century: Late Lessons from Early Warnings. London: Earthscan.

Jackson, Norman and Pippa Carter (2000). Rethinking Organizational Behaviour. Harlow: Pearson Education.

Jakubowski, Peter (1999). Demokratische Umweltpolitik. Eine institutionenökonomische Analyse Umweltpolitischer Zielfindung. Frankfurt am Main: Peter Lang.

Jakubowski, Peter (2000). political economic person contra homo oeconomicus. Mit PEP zu mehr Nachhaltigkeit. List Forum für Wirtschafts- und Finanzpolitik. Band 26, Heft 4, pp. 299–310.

Kindleberger, Charles P. (1958). International Economics, revd edn. Homewood, IL: Irwin.

Kindleberger, Charles P. (1962). Foreign Trade and the National Economy. New Haven, CT: Yale University Press.

Korten, David C. (2001). When Corporations Rule the World, 2nd edn. West Hartford, CT: Kumarian Press.

Mishan, Ezra J. (1971). Cost-Benefit Analysis. London: Allen & Unwin.

Mishan, Ezra J. (1980). How valid are economic evaluations of allocative changes? Journal of Economic Issues, Vol. 14, No. 1, pp. 143–61.

Myrdal, Gunnar (1978). Institutional economics. Journal of Economic Issues, Vol. 12, No. 4 pp. 771–83.

Siebenhüner, Bernd (2000). Homo sustinens – towards a conception of humans for the science of sustainability. Ecological Economics, Vol. 32, pp. 15–25.

Siebenhüner, Bernd (2001). Homo Sustinens. Auf dem Weg zu einem Menschenbild der Nachhaltigkeit. Marburg: Metropolis Verlag.

Söderbaum, Peter (1998). Stakeholders as political economic persons – on participation, responsibility and democracy. In Adelheid Biesecker, Wolfram Elsner and Klaus Grenzdörffer (eds), Ökonomie der Betroffenen und Mitwirkenden: Erweiterte Stakeholder-Prozesse. Pfaffenweiler: Centaurus, pp. 241–60.

Söderbaum, Peter (2000). Ecological Economics: A Political Economics Approach to Environment and Development. London: Earthscan.

World Bank (2001). Making Sustainable Commitments: An Environment Strategy for the World Bank. Summary. Washington, DC: World Bank.

World Commission on Dams (WCD) (2000). Dams and Development: A New Framework for Decision Making. London: Earthscan.

World Council of Churches (2001). Lead Us Not Into Temptation … Churches' Response to the Policies of International Financial Institutions. Geneva: WCC.

5

Changing Paradigms, Evolving Mandates, and Challenges for Faith and Development Partners

Katherine Marshall

The tragic events of September 11, 2001 (as well as other September 11 anniversaries, past and present) remind us of how interconnected we are in this world – our vulnerability and the preciousness of all life – yet how drastically differently we experience events and images.

The WCC, the IMF and the World Bank are engaged in an ambitious joint enterprise to explore, through dialogue over a two-year period, areas of common concern and belief, and areas of difference. Our underlying purpose could not be more important: it is to achieve both a better mutual understanding of our respective institutions and their work to fight poverty and strive for a more just world, and to explore how we can build on these understandings to forge stronger partnerships to achieve shared objectives. We, from the World Bank, have embarked on this process with the strong conviction that there is a powerful common core in the central objectives of our three institutions, though this common ground has tended too often in the past to be veiled behind different vocabulary, misunderstandings and unaddressed differences in approach. I draw continuing inspiration from the final metaphor put forward during our February encounter: that we should work to form a 'Fellowship of the Road'. While maintaining and accepting our very different approaches and programmes, nonetheless we join together as we move from place to place, along what we know and agree is a very dangerous road. We look to you as powerful allies (underlining that allies are both friends and critics) in working to meet the central challenges for humanity in this century.

I see the greatest challenges facing development practitioners and humans today much less as a confrontation of different paradigms or ideologies than as a complex set of actions to confront the varied, practical, and all-too-real challenges of poverty. The top challenges are low formal education enrolment; gender inequality; high child mortality and devastating maternal health statistics; HIV/AIDS, malaria, and other communicable diseases that plague and devastate the developing world; and developing countries stalled in their development path by burdens including high debt levels, weak institutions and corruption.

This chapter builds on initial reactions to Professor Peter Söderbaum's thought-provoking analysis of alternative contemporary options for and approaches to economic thinking, and its implications for the dialogue among the World Council of Churches, the IMF and the World Bank. His conclusions argue for changes in approach that put democracy and sustainable development at the centre of our discussions and action. Much in the analysis and ideologies that Professor Söderbaum presents and espouses echoes major themes that are part and parcel of the discussion and dialogue within the World Bank today. These are ideals for which the World Bank, as an institution and as a staff, from its most senior levels, are passionate advocates and proponents. I particularly welcome Professor Söderbaum's reflections on the complex topic of ethics as part of institutional and professional approaches.

I underscore that we simply do not accept many of the characterizations involved in the 'labelling' of World Bank thinking as framed within a neoliberal paradigm, both in general and in terms of specific definitions of 'neoliberal' that we have examined together. Thus, we welcome further discussion of this topic. It will be useful to reflect together on where we find real and current areas of disagreement, as well as reaffirming and clarifying the areas on which we all agree.

The World Bank is committed to a multi-sector, multi-partner approach to development, a development that encompasses sustainable, social, human ideas and ideals. We see room for a wide variety of approaches, and rich experience to learn from, both successful and unsuccessful. One lesson I and my colleagues take from past experience is an enhanced appreciation of the complexity of the development process. We have all been troubled and humbled by setbacks, as well as inspired by successes, and we are determined to learn from experience – our own and that of others. It is important to stress at the outset that we pride ourselves on our deep commitment to our underlying statement of purpose: 'Our dream is a world free of poverty' – or stated differently: 'Our aim is to fight poverty with passion and professionalism'.

An underlying theme for our dialogue is the impact and role of globalization and what it means for our roles and our work. We are as troubled as you by obvious negative facets of globalization. However, this phenomenon of globalization has many dimensions, good and bad. Globalization can be imagined as a canvas with two sides. One side is bright, multicoloured and positive. It includes the extraordinary technological advances that we all enjoy – the global 'hardware' of email, cell-phones and communications – and the opening of opportunities for so many to enjoy and benefit from the world's diverse riches. The other side is sombre, with global spread of dangers, disease and threats to the environment. We are also deeply concerned by the challenges to multilateralism, and agree on the need for creative, inspired, prophetic thinking about global governance.

We see great urgency, as well as great moral imperatives, in our common challenge. A great poet said: 'Ever at my back, I hear Time's winged chariot drawing near'. In far too many places we (as a global family) are not winning our central battle for a better world. In many meetings we are offered the poignant reminder of how many people contracted HIV, how many children have been orphaned, simply in the course of the discussion. Thus, we insist on the vital importance, working together and through a range of instruments, of what we term a 'scaling up' of efforts. An example: we know that medicines exist that can allow people with HIV/AIDS to live good lives for many years, yet we estimate that in Africa today, of 30 million infected by the HIV/AIDS virus, only some 20,000–50,000 currently have access to anti-retroviral therapy. Scaling up means scaling that gap. The Millennium Development Goals (MDGS) offer a useful global framework against which we can and should plan our action and which will allow us all to judge results and amend the course. The year 2015, the target date set by the United Nations and the global community to achieve the MDGs, is rapidly approaching and we have far, far to go to achieve what are in many respects quite minimal standards.

Isaiah Berlin observed that the world needs at least two kinds of leaders (and also institutions): hedgehogs and foxes. 'Hedgehogs' are consumed by one big idea, while 'foxes' know many things and understand the need for endlessly varied approaches to solve endlessly varied problems.[1] I fear that we are in many respects perceived by parts of your communities as a large neoliberal hedgehog! I see the World Bank very much as a fox, and indeed believe strongly we need to be a better, wiser, farther-seeing fox to cope with the extraordinarily complex, fast moving and changing, and critically important challenges of today and tomorrow. Ngozi Okonjo-Iweala, Nigeria's new finance minister, observed in her farewell admonition to her friends in the World Bank: 'It is a chaotic world, and it operates in real time'. We need to respond with great creativity, wisdom and urgency to the challenge.

EVOLUTION OF DEVELOPMENT CHALLENGES AND INSTITUTIONAL MANDATES

During the February 2003 WCC encounter, much discussion reflected on the evolution of the respective mandates of our three institutions since their creation. The backdrop was how the major global changes which have transformed the world have affected formal and informal mandates, and particularly how we have lived the evolving approaches to the 'developing' world. Today, we might frame that challenge more sharply as the fight against poverty and for greater social justice. This section reflects on some of the specific changes that have affected the World Bank over the past decades. In sum, we have lived the same history, but we have lived it rather differently. One of the benefits we hope will stem from our encounters is to ensure that we are debating the issues and institutions of today, not yesterday, informed and inspired by a historical perspective on the journey we have traversed and the lessons we have learned from it.

There are two critical arguments. The first is that the changes in the World Bank, both formal and informal, amount to a transformation. We can safely guess that the founders of the World Bank, who debated its mandate and structure in 1944, would scarcely recognize the institution of today. While the Bank's mandate has evolved continuously throughout its history, the changes over the last decade have been particularly significant; in many respects, the Bank can be seen as in a state of 'permanent structural adjustment' as it responds to the dynamic of change.

The second point is that these changes have come about as part of the remarkable shifts in thinking about development and, more broadly, the set of phenomena that together are termed 'globalization'. While the Bank's experience has shaped this thinking, it is much better seen as part of the backdrop of change in national and international institutions, the evolution of global governance mechanisms, and sociopolitical changes at national and international levels.

The discussions of February (and particularly Rob van Drimmelen's remarkable paper on ecumenical approaches to development) brought out the rich experience and prophetic role of the WCC on many issues. An underlying argument from the WCC, which we have understood, is that the WCC in its thinking and action came to new understandings of many development issues, especially those we term social and environmental issues, well ahead of the World Bank. You may therefore view changes in Bank rhetoric and work as late and wrought with some reluctance. We appreciate this perspective, even as we sometimes disagree on chronologies. I am sure you will agree also that in many areas the World Bank has been an intellectual and action leader in addressing development issues.

We came away from our discussions in February with the insight that our three institutions have been shaped by many of the same extraordinary challenges, even as all three were founded on many of the same underlying hypotheses about global development and institutions (including, notably, the process that forged the Universal Declaration of Human Rights) that emerged in the final years of the Second World War.

RECONSTRUCTION AND DEVELOPMENT

It is useful to recall that the World Bank was very much part of the effort to design, in the final years of the Second World War and its immediate aftermath, a new architecture for global relationships that would prevent future wars and support reconstruction. We know well that the challenges of the 'Third World' were perceived then, but quite dimly, and not with a central priority in the 'architectural' design of the multilateral governance institutions. Thus, the World Bank, or the International Bank for Reconstruction and Development as it was termed when it was founded in 1944, was largely geared to help reconstruct a Europe and an Asia devastated by war, with a focus on infrastructure development. The World Bank's weighted voting structure is very much a legacy of the thinking and negotiations of this period (though it has in practice evolved quite significantly over the years).

The World Bank opened its doors, therefore, with loans to war-damaged countries, including France, Italy and Japan. These were large loans for reconstruction. The Bank's history took an early detour, however, as it became clear that resources and institutional mechanisms were vastly inadequate to meet real needs. The Marshall Plan in 1947 essentially took from it the European reconstruction mandate and left the World Bank with a focus on development (which had been almost an afterthought in early discussions of the World Bank). That focus has sharpened and deepened ever since.

The first decades of the Bank saw an institution that earned a reputation for careful financial and technical appraisal. One benefit derived from this early institutional investment, which is still important today, is the Bank's financial reputation. This allows it to borrow on highly favourable terms on international financial markets, and to pass on the benefits to its borrowers. Another benefit has come through the discipline of the appraisal process, and its fiduciary tools, such as auditing and procurement procedures, both for the Bank's staff, and for borrowing countries. In this period, the overall portfolio of loans, many for infrastructure and large-scale agriculture, reflected the assumption that development would come through transfers of physical and financial capital, with the Bank playing essentially a catalytic role. The creation of the International Finance Corporation

(IFC) in 1956 reflected efforts to give more focus and new instruments to what was seen as the critical role of private investment.

THE TUMULT OF THE 1960S

The 1960s saw far-ranging changes, most prominently the creation of the International Development Association (IDA), that was to offer the poorest countries loans with highly concessional terms. The first IDA loans (known as credits) were approved in 1961, to Honduras, India, Sudan and Chile. Over the next decade, the World Bank's work (and this now encompassed IBRD and IDA) expanded into new areas, including education and agriculture. An important legacy from this period, an important characteristic of the World Bank which we may want to discuss, is the focus on numbers (statistics), used with the objective of ensuring fairness and as one bulwark against engaging in political interventions and judgements. The need to ration highly desirable IDA funds (0 per cent interest, 50 years to repay) led, for example, to careful criteria for allocation, based on relative poverty, population and performance – the latter redefined over time as the concept expanded. It now includes governance as well as performance in using funds. Many other areas were quantified – I recall that the World Bank's President, Robert McNamara, would not accept that it was too hard to put numbers on issues, setting teams, for example, scrambling to justify a rural water supply project by putting a quantitative value on the time women saved when they did not need to carry water each day.

THE MCNAMARA ERA AND THE 1970S

The Bank has been shaped by ideas, the challenges and opportunities presented by its member countries, and by its leaders and staff. This March, Jim Wolfensohn organized a dinner to pay tribute to the leadership of Bob McNamara, President from 1968 to 1981. McNamara's era saw transformations of the World Bank in many respects: rapid increases in size, a move to a much more visible and forceful stance on advocacy for development issues, and the addition of new areas, including health, nutrition, population, and a strong focus on disciplined research (primarily, but not exclusively, in economic fields). McNamara articulated strongly the poverty goals of the Bank. He spoke of the 'lowest 40 per cent' and challenged all to new rural and urban development strategies. When he left in 1981 the World Bank was a very different institution than it was in 1968. It was a much bigger player, more diverse in its staff, working in a much larger group of countries, more visible and thus more controversial, and with a bold and demanding culture and vision. I still remember the quote from Bernard Shaw in McNamara's last annual meeting speech: "You see things and you ask 'why'. I dream things and I ask 'why not?'"[2]

CRISES AND RETHINKING IN THE 1980S AND EARLY 1990S

The history of the early decades, while rather distant now in many respects, serves as an important backdrop for the major world changes and challenges of the 1980s and early 1990s, which saw two historic developments which transformed the World Bank again. The first was a succession of economic and financial crises –

mainly oil and debt, but also crises which might be termed crises of ideology and governance, which brought countries to their knees, in many cases time and time again. The second was the collapse of the Soviet bloc, bringing new challenges of 'transition' that echoed all over the world. It also brought a large number of new countries as members of the World Bank. The World Bank's character was altered in many ways thereafter, not only because of the very different challenges presented by the transition states, but also by the global changes in power relations that came with the end of the Cold War. The World Bank has become very much a global, 'world' institution (44 members in 1944, 184 member countries today), which it clearly was not before.

There was a third major change, which was not fully apparent at the time, and which also posed deep challenges to the Bank and led to a cascading set of changes: the mounting critique of the World Bank's impact on the environment and stance on environmental issues, which was followed by a complex and important array of new policies and structures. The process of challenge and response helped to bring about new thinking and paradigms in areas far beyond the environment per se.

I will dwell briefly here on the World Bank's response to the economic crises, which at least in the early years was called structural adjustment. This has particular significance because it is the Bank's work in this area that seems to have coloured its reputation in many circles, and is thus important background for discussions on macroeconomic models and ideologies. Some observations may be quite familiar, while others are more personal hypotheses (born of my own experience):

1   The new forms of lending that evolved in response to the economic crises that beset nation after nation were very different from the 'project' approach which supported specific investments and which had so much dominated World Bank lending throughout its first decades of operation (and which still today constitute the significant majority of its lending). The Bank was lending essentially for balance of payments or budget support, with large, concentrated disbursements of funds to the government. This led sometimes to a preference for and even dependence on such transfers, which posed problems because they were always justified as exceptional in the early years.

2   The World Bank's economic advice came to be much more directly tied to both specific adjustment loans and to the overall judgements on creditworthiness which determined lending levels. Much of the early experience with conditions for these new loans (which were controversial and required exceptional justifications) was based on the understanding that the reform programmes were to be quick, sharp changes which would put the economy back on a 'normal' growth path. This, plus the crisis atmosphere in which many were designed and negotiated, gave a 'shock therapy' character to many programmes and operations.

3   The approaches and underlying justifications for 'structural adjustment' lending changed fundamentally over time. As it became clear that many

countries would need successive reforms and loans, the structure of policy-based lending changed. One phenomenon, as conditions were not met, was a tendency to a more complex set of conditionalities. As time went on there was more focus on the social impact of adjustment. Finally, more and more the programmes came to be seen as longer term, focused on 'second generation' reforms, which were recognized to be more complex. The links between the macroeconomic and sectoral lending and specific investment projects became much clearer and more explicit, today a central focus of the strategic framework for World Bank work in countries, which is known as the Country Assistance Strategy (CAS).

4   The new lending changed relationships with many countries, sometimes in a favourable way, other times leading to great tensions. There was also active discussion with the World Bank's Executive Directors about the nature, conditions and directions of such lending.

5   The first loans were generally very secret, with little known about their terms and the agreed conditions. This has changed over time, so that today there is an appreciation that reform programmes must be grounded in public understanding and support. Much more information about the programmes and specific loan instruments is in the public domain.

6   With this new instrument, the view of project lending came to change. A first realization was that no project could succeed or last in the face of poor, particularly abysmal, economic management. The second was an unrelated but linked realization that the 'patchwork quilt' of projects financed by numerous donors had many damaging effects, including inter alia overlapping – even contradictory – objectives, excessive demands for paperwork, poor resource use and great burdens on recipient countries. This fuelled efforts for rationalization of aid and moves to 'programmatic' lending (for example, common programmes engaging most or all donor partners to support national and country-led transport or education sector programmes).

7   The new lending led to a complex set of new relationships with the IMF – some positive, but also with some rather well-known tensions. It changed relations with many other institutions, particularly as several also became involved in 'quick disbursing lending' and sought to frame their development interventions more explicitly in a common national strategic framework.

This summary suggests two important conclusions. First, there has been important continuing evolution in thinking and approaches for 'quick disbursing lending'. Generally, it is more likely to be termed 'programmatic' lending today, but it takes many forms. Much lending associated with debt relief, for example, takes this form. Second, the balance between 'project' and 'quick disbursing' lending and underlying policies has altered dramatically and with it the work of the Bank. Today, we see the two as very much linked and complementary, with the links set out in the Country Assistance Strategy.

'EARTHQUAKES' OF THE 1990s

Many fundamental and far-reaching events have shaken the World Bank over the past decade. Our institution, like yours, has been directly and deeply affected by the rapid changes in the world, including, inter alia, wars and conflict, deep economic crises, new approaches to social policy, rethinking of practice and social justice around national debt, the HIV/AIDS pandemic, the globalization debates and protests, and new thinking and action on issues of governance, including the phenomenon of corruption. A deep crisis of confidence in the World Bank centred around its fiftieth anniversary, and had major ricochet effects inside and outside the institution. The Jubilee 2000 debt campaign was another event with great historic significance for thinking and action on development issues. Building on a continuing construction of case-by-case action increasingly set in a debate on (and framework of) evolving policies, progress was made (albeit somewhat fitfully and too slowly) in living up to the objective and moral guarantee that effective national programmes should not be impaired by the legacy of excessive debt burdens. The Poverty Reduction Strategy Paper framework, aimed to put the fight against poverty at the strategic heart for countries and multilateral institutions and to provide practical ways to direct resources to social programmes, is an important outcome.

An important factor in the changes that have transformed the World Bank is the leadership of Jim Wolfensohn as President of the World Bank: he has personally driven many changes, among them new openness to civil society, including the world of religion, a focus on a Comprehensive Development Framework which explicitly recognizes both the vital importance of economic and social factors and the needed richness of partnerships to achieve our objectives, and, most recently, a commitment to engage with youth.

The World Bank has thus seen very dramatic changes in organization, policy, personnel, and in many respects, ethos. Living through these decades of history myself, it is dramatic how far the Bank has moved towards a different balance between economic agendas on one side and what might be characterized as environmental and social agendas on the other. Human, social and sustainable development have become core concepts for our work at the Bank. It became not only acceptable, but also crucial, to think about cultures and specific country and regional contexts. These elements shape effective development that we know to be more in tune with the human experience, but they are also more complicated to define than strict economic development. These development concepts are differently defined from institution to institution, and they evolve – shaped by forces within the Bank and from outside, forces which push the Bank towards themes of inclusiveness and holistic development, themes that are differently interpreted and enacted in diverse ways within our institution. These forces are pushing the institution in new directions, putting people first in the development process (not as a matter of rhetoric but as a matter of human transformation at its best), empowering the voiceless and the powerless, and being explicit about 'who is who' in development (acknowledging indigenous peoples and all other minorities, being more transparent about the winners and losers of development).

THE WORLD BANK TODAY – ITS 'MODEL' AND 'MODE'

So what is the institution today? What does it do? What is the underlying 'model' it follows (if any)? What has it learned from its experience? And what direction is it taking? These questions constitute an important element in the encounter process in which the World Bank, the IMF and the WCC have engaged. The process offers the chance both for introspection and for seeing our familiar institution with the eyes of those approaching it from different positions. We value the opportunity to engage in this dialogue, on realities and perceptions, as well as on the different views seen from different perspectives (in the metaphor of the blind men feeling the elephant and describing very different creatures).

A central feature and asset of the World Bank is its involvement in many different domains of the complex field of development, and a central challenge is to see the linkages and emerging issues. Briefly, I see five main 'domains':

1. Macroeconomic dialogue and support: the overall framework and its capacity to ensure stability and allow and encourage growth; also, its effectiveness in supporting poverty reduction strategies.
2. Programmes at the micro level, including the exciting work termed 'community driven development', but also a wide range of activities centring on poor communities and institutions.
3. Engagement in a wide range of sectors, often over decades (education, transport, energy, agriculture, urban development, etc.).
4. Engagement with cross-cutting issues like environment, gender, private sector strategies and capacity-building initiatives.
5. Strategic thinking about long-term trends and goals, in the form of 'visions'.

In each country where the World Bank supports the development process, these different facets are woven together in a strategic framework, in a comprehensive and balanced programme. Here are some facets of the institution as we see them:

- The World Bank is a multifaceted, multi-disciplinary institution. It is highly complex – perhaps a truism, but a true one. The staff comes from all over the world, and most academic disciplines are represented. Diversity is a key and explicit objective.
- The Bank operates very differently in different countries, deliberately. In many respects the most informative way to see the Bank is to look at its country programmes, individually and in aggregate. To take two examples, look how the World Bank programmes in two neighbouring countries, Mozambique and South Africa, differ, because the countries' needs are so different. The World Bank's dialogue on education spans the range from discussion of the most sophisticated science institutions (the Millennium Science Institutions) to advocacy for the importance of universal primary education and the practical obstacles that stop parents from sending girls to school.
- The diversity of 'products' is important. These range from large adjustment loans ($3 billion in South Korea, for example) to a multitude of community-driven development operations, post-conflict work, social funds, and Learning and Innovation loans that approach the development

challenge from a very different vantage point. The diversity of 'knowledge products' is at least as great.

- The Bank's advocacy role has increasing importance. Witness two recent examples: the work in preparation for the WTO/Cancún discussions, and the work on links between conflict and resources.
- The increasing complexity of partnerships is a critical characteristic of the institution. We work with a very wide range of institutions, some in formal arrangements involving finance, others more akin to alliances.
- The information and communications role of the Bank deserves attention – its research and other papers, including the Development Gateway.

The World Bank faces many challenges, and these are the topic of intense debate inside as well as outside the institution. Briefly, some of the topics which we see as critical current issues for dialogue and action include the following. This may suggest elements for our future agenda and dialogue process:

- Governance issues, including how far the World Bank (in the light of its mandate not to interfere in the domestic political affairs of its member countries) can and should go in addressing political issues that are linked to development. Action on decentralization at country level, putting meaning into the objective of empowerment, and approaches to the problem of corruption are other important governance issues.
- Continuing debate around the primacy of growth as a central objective and what 'pro-poor' growth means, in theory and practice.
- Debt: underlying issues of the role and appropriate levels of borrowing, concept of sustainable debt, debts versus grants, crisis management and restructuring.
- 'Unbundling' the adjustment debates and discussions around macroeconomic policies.
- Economists and their institutional role, as well as evolution within the discipline of economics towards more focus on sustainability and institutions – how is this reflected in practice, and how can the World Bank maximize the benefit it derives from its multidisciplinary and multi-sector team character?
- Participation: its character and limits, including the management of processes of public consultation and engagement.
- Disclosure policies (what further information about the World Bank's work should be disclosed to the public and when).
- Debates around 'safeguard policies'[3]: are these appropriately defined? What future direction should they take?
- What the Bank can and should do to support the poorest countries and countries in conflict (what we term the LICUS countries – Low Income Countries under Stress). The irony is that countries which do not have strong leadership and policy frameworks, and which face war and conflict, are often the poorest, yet are the hardest to reach and help with most current development instruments.
- Whether the World Bank's role is well tuned to the needs of middle-income countries.

- New thinking on corporate social responsibility, both for the World Bank as an institution and as a new force shaping private sector engagement.
- 'Ownership' demands and issues (the essential need for countries and institutions to own and believe in programmes if they are to work) versus global agendas which reflect mandates and global experience.
- 'Selectivity': there are many who argue that the World Bank's mandate is too broad – nigh impossible – and suggest that we need to exercise more selectivity in the issues we address and sector programmes we support. This can run counter to the fundamental insight behind the Comprehensive Development Framework: that issues and problems are linked in countless ways. It is, for example, a central reason for my own job and work programme – that without a better understanding of the world of religion, and without better dialogue with those who see development ethics issues in different ways, we cannot succeed. You should be aware, though, that this work is among the first on the list of areas suggested by some World Bank critics which do not deserve priority (my only satisfaction is that it displaces gender, sometimes).
- Rhetoric/reality/diversity. We are well aware of the critique that there is a gap between the World Bank's rhetoric and the realities on the ground. This is complicated by the fact that the World Bank operates so differently in different places – its real decentralization is an important characteristic. We also recognize the risks of a 'time lag' between the adoption of policies and their practical implementation at country level, one of the reasons for the strong focus in the World Bank today on 'implementation' and 'results'. There is also a reverse phenomenon – that some policies and insights are implemented first 'on the ground', with policy and formal statements following the reality.
- Pragmatism is a key characteristic of the World Bank – how can and should this be managed?
- Our communications are improving and we see communication as critical – a sophisticated view that involves dialogue, listening, and hearing – but we still tend to talk in very technical terms in too many settings.
- The balance between a focus on poverty and the poorest communities versus a broader social agenda. In some areas the central focus on poverty and only the very poorest segments of the society can obscure the central objective of a policy framework that is inclusive and focuses on the social welfare of all parts of the community.

NEOLIBERAL PARADIGMS

We do not accept the characterization of the World Bank as driven by a neoliberal model, as reflected in some WCC documents that we have examined together. Our aim is to put people at the centre of development, and we firmly believe in diverse approaches that must be driven by those affected. We also hold firmly to the view that 'different worlds' and different models are both possible and desirable, and adapt programmes consciously to the wishes and needs of each country. We have learned much about the vital importance of participation, and are working in countless ways to develop better approaches along these lines (termed the 'empowerment agenda') and to use them well. We see this as linked to better governance (though we rarely talk of democracy per se, as it can suggest that we are advocating a particular political system). The Bank staff includes many economists, but also large numbers of staff in other disciplines, with the balance changing. We have active debates about what is best, and, increasingly, the ethical issues involved are discussed more explicitly than they were in the past. In sum, we do not offer a 'development paradigm' or 'mandate' or 'ideology' for the taking. The modus operandi is to work from a holistic model of development and to keep working at development as well as we know how. We know that we do not have all of the answers, and we are very much learning as we go along in this development work. In the spirit of setting out an agenda for future discussion, I highlight a few points on the 'neoliberal global economic strategy', as articulated in WCC documents and which formed a basis for discussions on the subject at the February encounter. My preliminary ideas and reactions follow the WCC 'definition'.[4]

- 'Turn exports into the main source of economic growth.' While increasing revenues and looking to exports to boost growth is often a national objective supported by the World Bank, rarely is a pure export-led growth strategy the driving force of a national strategy. This topic highlights the importance of dialogue on issues around trade reform more generally, including a focus on experience with trade reform and the benefits and issues of open versus protected economies: witness the debates in Cancún.

- 'Reduce the scope of state economic power and maximize privatization.' This seems a caricature of the complex issues and debates around reforms of state roles (including decentralization and modernization). To be very clear, it is never and should never be the objective of World Bank advice and support simply to maximize privatization.

- 'Give absolute precedence to the preservation of macroeconomic objectives and policies, while neglecting social costs to people in their daily life. Ironically many economists call these core human concerns "externalities".' No, human capital is often the 'absolute priority' and social issues are front and centre.

- 'Search for profitability and efficiency in the short term, instead of attending to long-term sustainable approaches to economic and social well-being.' Absolutely not; sustainability and medium- to long-term ramifications are at the core of the World Bank's thinking.

- 'Eliminate impediments to the free mobility of capital across the planet.' This is an overstatement of policies and approach, and the topic currently engages active debate and rethinking.

Three central and live issues seem worth putting at the centre of our agendas:

1   Growth: how to achieve growth, is it indeed essential, and what is the practical implication of the aim of 'pro-poor' and 'sustainable' growth?
2   Articulation and discussion of alternative approaches: what would they look like? Where do we see them in practice?
3   Implications of a diversity of approaches in our diverse world.

CHALLENGES FOR FAITH AND DEVELOPMENT PARTNERS

The World Bank is moving in many ways to address more explicitly the many normative aspects of development: our increasing focus on the full gamut of issues for poverty and on institutions as they serve and affect poor communities draws us powerfully in this direction, as do the live debates around globalization issues. Other examples of how this work translates into practice are the programmes for governance (including support for anti-corruption programmes, empowerment, and justice system reform programmes). Ethical, normative, moral and spiritual values are of great interest to World Bank staff throughout the institution. As an illustration, a Values in Development group has met for several decades each Friday morning to reflect on issues of concern and to explore possible avenues towards solutions.

A particular area of focus is on bringing the world of development into closer dialogue and partnership with the world of religious and faith organizations. While interfaith work and social and development work within individual faiths obviously have very deep roots and ancient origins, the effort to span the divides (institutional, practical and intellectual) separating the worlds of development practitioners and faith communities has a more recent origin. The discussions at the 2000 UN Millennium Summit, which involved religious and development leaders, and the pursuit of the World Faiths Development Dialogue (WFDD) (since 1998), illustrate this awakening interest in many common objectives and concerns. Development and faith leaders at the international level have focused more and more on the range of questions about the roles of religion and interfaith dialogue in the critical areas identified as those which must be addressed to end poverty: education, delivery of healthcare services, water and sanitation, the roles of women and men in society, social cohesion, and other areas. This dialogue puts a spotlight on questions about faith leaders as agents of change, and the lessons to be learned by and from different partners in addressing society's challenges. Coupled with the objectives of social and economic transformation, the overlap and common ground of shared interests are woven in countless ways.

There is still much scope for strengthening the partnership between faith and development organizations. This reflects in part a traditional divide between these two worlds. As we know, there remains scepticism on both sides about working together, reflecting different values, different norms, different languages, different approaches. But the role of community and civil society is clearly fundamental to success and sustainability. And the role of faith-based groups is especially vital. As you well know, many basic issues that are central to the world of development – poverty alleviation, a rights-based approach to education, social justice, welfare, and the meaning of progress – are core issues in all of the major religious traditions, with intellectual and moral roots that can be traced back thousands of years. Theologians from every religion have grappled with the why's and how's of poverty and misery. For centuries, faith institutions have played a pivotal role in providing services to the poor, and in working to overcome the underlying roots of poverty. In short, the international development community is coming to a much clearer consensus that development and faith leaders should be working together.

The World Bank is thus much more open today to the world of faith leaders and religion, a world which has much to teach development practitioners about how best to respond to the poor. Alfredo spoke of effective development mandates needing ethical and moral groundings in order to provide space for self-realization. In many parts of the world, churches and leaders of many faith traditions are providing this very space for the poor, at the individual and community levels: self-realization in the form of participation, ownership, empowerment, information, satisfaction of basic material needs, community-based approaches, access to justice, and more. Faith communities are important service providers and community leaders and have made remarkable inroads in improving the lives of the poor, allowing them to go beyond a material dimension into a spiritual dimension: to the worlds of identity, sharing, caring, love, inner wisdom and the sacred.

The Bank recognizes the great potential of partnerships with faith organizations, for practical reasons for extending the reach of our work and also to pursue these connections between material and spiritual worlds and the self-realization of individuals and institutions. The Development Dialogue on Values and Ethics in the World Bank is charged to explore this terrain, to evaluate the current and potential relationships between the World Bank and faith leaders and religious organizations. Closer collaboration between the Bank and faith institutions can include the Poverty Reduction Strategy Papers (PRSP) and Country Assistance Strategy (CAS) consultations, World Development Report consultations, education (in the context of the Education for All initiative), and HIV/AIDS strategies and programmes at country levels. The Bank needs to be keenly aware of the sensitivities involved and the important frontiers between 'church' and 'state', yet development practitioners and the institution as a whole cannot turn a blind eye to the vital institutions, experience, insights and ideas that come from faith institutions like the World Council of Churches.

DEVELOPMENT: MOVING FROM DISCUSSION OF PARADIGMS TO THE BANK'S WORK

Our work at the World Bank is centred around the task of bringing our resources, energy and technical expertise to bear on crucial development problems, supporting the implementation of comprehensive poverty reduction strategies, and striving to become more reflective about our activities. Crucially, our organization will be tested, not by which paradigm it employs, but by the extent to which we are able to achieve the benchmarks (those set for ourselves and those that are set externally) in realizing our vision of a world free of poverty. A vital set of benchmarks are the Millennium Development Goals.

The September 2000 Millennium Declaration by world leaders proclaimed: 'We will spare no effort to free our fellow men, women and children from the abject and dehumanizing conditions of extreme poverty, to which more than a billion are currently subjected.' The Millennium Development Goals reflect a new determination to mobilize energy, resources and passion behind tangible, quantified formulations of imperatives. The year 2015 is the date when we are committed to judge how well we have done in defeating the ancient scourges of want, ignorance, hunger and strife. The goals are straightforward: halve poverty, halt the spread of communicable diseases, ensure that all children go to school and at least finish primary school, work to protect and improve the environment. Global leaders and institutions (like the World Bank) are committed to judging their performance against these goals, as are nations and their leaders.

How will we reach these goals? How do we establish a system in which we are truly accountable to poor people and to our environment (as well as to our member governments)?

- The most critical factor is a common sense of purpose and will. This in turn calls for action at a scale we have not witnessed in the past, and new and dynamic forms of partnerships among all the actors concerned.
- Some institutional mechanisms help us with this. The Operations Evaluation Department (OED), an independent unit with the World Bank, reviews every completed Bank project (all evaluations are available on the World Bank website). Increasing transparency and access to information through the Internet will mean that more people are able to observe and evaluate the Bank's activities, and in this way the Bank is made publicly accountable.
- In terms of mechanisms for accountability and governance, we are accountable to the board of governors and, on everyday management, to the board of executive directors, who are appointed by the executive branch of governments. We operate on the assumption that these governments are representative, and face considerable difficulties, practical and ethical, in addressing issues for poor communities in countries where governance is a central problem and issue.
- It is and will be useful to focus on areas where there are gaps between rhetoric and reality 'on the ground', as such examples can point to practical ways to improve operations and the institution itself.

Of utmost importance is the need for the World Bank to reaffirm constantly its commitment to honouring the lives and integrity of the poor. We need to make sure that words like participation, inclusion and empowerment are not only buzzwords around the office and in our publications, but also words that drive our work and remind us of what matters most for the poor.

Notes

1   Quoted by Gareth Evans, *International Herald Tribune*, September 11, 2003.

2   This is a Bernard Shaw quotation, often useb by John and Robert Kennedy.

3   The World Bank Group (which includes the Bank, IFC and MIGA) has been a leader among development institutions in promoting attention to sustainable development. For more than 20 years the Bank has had policies requiring that potentially adverse environmental impacts and selected social impacts of its investment projects be identified, avoided, or minimized and mitigated; and in 1997, Bank Management designated this specific set of policies as "safeguard policies" to stress their importance

for achieving its environmental and social objectives and for enhancing the quality of its operations' (from World Bank website). The ten policies address primarily environmental and social policies, including protection of cultural property.

4   WCC, "Economic Globalization: Deepening Challenge for Christians", Geneva, October 1998.

6

Response to the World Bank

Ulrich Moeller

I am not an economist. I am a theologian and a member of the governing board of the Protestant Church of Westfalia, a united church, one of the large regional churches within the Protestant Church in Germany. This means that I speak as a Christian from the North, in a society where the people (as well as the churches) are still more on the side of the winners than the victims of globalization, although more and more of us are experiencing the negative impacts of deregulation and privatization within the present neoliberal project.

My point of departure is not a neutral one. As a church representative and as an individual, I am actively involved in the ecumenical process for globalizing justice, with the aim of establishing an economy in the service of life. I give my response to the World Bank contribution of Katherine Marshall (chapter 5, above) from this specific perspective. I think we all appreciate the personal engagement and credibility with which she has tried to push forward with the important aims and values we may share and agree upon. This provides a good basis for dialogue, which can only be fruitful if we are open and search for mutual understanding.

BASIC THEOLOGICAL PERSPECTIVES ON GLOBALIZATION

Today's international finance markets are the result of the liberalization, deregulation and privatization of larger and larger parts of an increasingly global economy. How do churches respond to the dominant project of globalization and its consequences for people and nature?

We confess in our faith: 'The earth belongs to God, the creation and all who live in it' (Psalm 24:1). Liberty, therefore, according to the Christian tradition, is not maximization of our own benefit; rather, it is our commitment as co-workers of God to give a foretaste to everyone of what it means to live the promised 'life in abundance'. From this perspective, the scandal of worldwide injustice is the central challenge when it comes to shaping global development responsibly.

Challenged by the cry of excluded and deprived people in the South, an ecumenical journey of confession and committed action has begun, to which the WCC, the WARC, the LWF and regional ecumenical councils in all continents are joined. There is no space here to elaborate on this very important process, in which a growing consensus between different church communities is becoming visible. However, this process always has two dimensions:

1   The committed witness of the churches themselves. They understand that economic injustice and ecological destruction is a matter of faith itself, which requires a common witness of the ecumenical communion of churches in word and deed.

2   Practical steps at all levels, including cooperation with other international organizations and partners. Therefore, when the 1997 General

Assembly of the World Alliance of Reformed Churches called upon its member churches for this committed process, it also asked 'to initiate in cooperation with other Christian world communions and the World Council of Churches a dialogue with the World Bank, the IMF and WTO with the goal that they review their policies and actions in the light of their adverse effect on the people of developing countries.'

God's promise of the fullness of life, his justice as the basis for justice on earth, and his option for the poor and excluded are our guiding principles. 'If a member of the body of Christ suffers, all members suffer' (1 Corinthians 12:26). There has thus been intensive discussion in the worldwide ecumenical movement since the middle of the 1990s at least, with agreement that injustice and the ongoing destruction of nature contradicts the core of the gospel and challenges the witness of the church. There is a growing ecumenical consensus that the predominant neoliberal economic framework has unacceptable theological implications and ethical consequences. This demands both a firm confessing stance and a prophetic voice. It is a necessary implication of our belief in God that we should seek dialogue and cooperation with all those who are committed to explore ways towards a form of development which is consistent with God's household and his promise of the fullness of life without exclusion.

DIFFERENT APPROACHES

This ecumenical stance views economic matters in the light of faith and follows God's preferential option for the poor as a basic theological paradigm. Is this compatible with contemporary predominant approaches to the international financial order? I shall try to answer this question by following the proposals of Martin Büscher and Lukas Menkhoff, authors of a recently published essay called 'Justice and Efficiency'.[1] They describe neoliberalism as aiming at efficiency without justice.

Today's international financial markets are the result of the liberalization, deregulation and privatization of more and more sectors of the economy. What is the (implicit) business ethic behind this liberalization policy?

The key category in discussion about international financial markets is efficiency, which has changed from one end among many into an end in itself, and its non-economic consequences are not the subject of widespread reflection. In this respect, efficiency is a category without ethical content. Efficiency at any cost increases the predominance of purely economic ideas at the expense of other values. This leads to an overestimation of the economy, as if it represented a worldview. Theologically speaking, so-called 'market justice' turns into a kind of idolatry, claiming sacrifices from among its victims —the weak, the exploited and the excluded. Ethically and theologically, this is totally unacceptable and requires the church to resist.

Büscher and Menkhoff describe three ethical concepts aimed at overcoming this shortcoming:

1   Participatory justice (a largely economic view)
2   Justice of results (different critics)
3   Justice for the poorest of the poor (in particular, church institutions)

Participatory justice

The main thrust of this view – largely argued in economic terms – is to design participation into economic competition. The basic idea is this: a market is only effective if all suitable participants have free access to it. Only those who are able to participate effectively in the market fulfil its minimum requirements. 'Weak' participants, being exposed to the market, can only lose in relative terms: this would not be just. Accordingly, developing countries have partially to be isolated from international financial markets. This requires both the inclusion of macro governance and a time-lag in terms of reforms in industrialized and developing countries. As all parties affected should be involved, and with the right of co-determination, the political consequence is to strengthen developing countries' participatory rights in international organizations that help shape the overall conditions of the international economic order. In particular, this leads to demands for such measures with regard to the international financial organizations.

Justice of results

Currently, the world economy 'punishes' the inefficient use of capital by withdrawing capital. This policy has dramatic consequences for the tens of millions of people living in abject poverty (e.g. the new poverty in Southeast Asia resulting from the Asian crisis). Ethically, it is unacceptable to subject people's entire existence to the criterion of economic efficiency and therefore indirectly to a maximization of the material standard of living. Other values are expressly stated as equal in rank. Aiming for a 'justice of results' therefore implies that free financial markets be given precise limits; that is, emphasis on macroeconomic governance, including the following elements:

- More resolute governmental cooperation to provide financial markets with political leadership.
- The volatility of prices on financial markets is to be reduced by means of the introduction of a transaction tax.
- Controls of international capital transactions are to provide national policy makers with more scope for action compared with market participants. This also includes debt release for the poorest countries, where the burden of debt threatens the very existence of the poor.

Thus, the regulatory instruments of financial market policy are to create the preconditions for ensuring capital markets do not just follow their own logic, but function meaningfully and efficiently in the interest of just results, based on political will.

Justice for the poorest of the poor

The ethical concept of the option for the poor focuses on the (economic) effect of policies on the poor in a given society. Under this approach, in order for reforms of the international financial order to be ethically justifiable, they have to benefit the poor.

Compared with the current debate about more or less efficiency, this perspective raises a fundamentally different question. In order to improve the situation of the poor, it is not enough simply to reform the international financial order. We must go beyond that, to question the distribution of power and wealth within society. This approach addresses the social system, the participation of individuals and compensation for different (potentially self-induced) fates.

The market basically knows no justice nor mercy, but rewards the strong (efficient) and punishes the weak (inefficient). Therefore, the only way to protect the weak is to regulate the markets.

> A reform proposal oriented to an option for the poor is therefore based on a strong International Monetary Fund. Only a supranational institution is able to regulate the market such that the goals of the poor are also being 'heard' – a feature that tends to reflect the idea of participatory justice – or that these goals are even realized by means of explicit measures 'against' market results – a feature that tends to represent the option for the poor.[2]

Consequently, this approach results in a far-reaching reform of international financial institutions such as the IMF and World Bank: 'Their task would shift from economic efficiency criteria towards the absolute goal of poverty reduction in terms of macroeconomic stabilization and funding of development activities.'[3] This implies a clear shift in decision-making powers in these institutions towards states with the largest populations of poor people. However, financial market policy within this concept is only one important part of an economic policy in the service of life, oriented towards the criteria of sustainability.

QUESTIONS AND CHALLENGES FOR THE WORLD BANK

Before I come to my questions and challenges for the World Bank, I want to provide an example to show the specific background to a major problem concerning dialogue between IFIs and the churches. It may help to explain why it is not easy to establish common ground, even if we seem to share many concerns.

The IMF and World Bank work for the liberalization of capital markets. The World Bank only allocates loans if the country concerned makes an agreement with the IMF. In turn, the IMF is the authority which provides needed loans in times of economic difficulty, when other governments and banks will not provide finance. Therefore, for other potential lenders, a country is creditworthy only on the basis of a positive examination by the IMF. It is a prerequisite for a positive examination that a country should have submitted to the structural adjustment programmes (SAPs) drawn up by the IMF together with the World Bank. These regulations orientate themselves in accordance with the so-called Washington Agreement, with the aim of 'household stabilization' by means of reduced expenditure and liberalization of the economy. This has led to a worldwide neoliberal reorganization of society and production and labour markets since the 1990s. Deregulation of labour markets for many millions of employees worldwide has led to a dramatic deterioration in conditions of employment. It is transnational corporations who particularly profit from these developments.

Due to the dept trap in which poor countries find themselves, again and again they are forced to negotiate new loans with the IMF and World Bank. As these loans are bound to the conditions of SAPs, the IMF and World Bank are forcing poor countries to the one-sided liberalization of trade. At the same time, the powerful industrialized countries which dominate the IFIs use customs duties to protect their markets against imports from the same poor countries, which through the IFIs they force to be exposed to market competition.

According to UNCTAD, this unfair treatment of developing countries leads to losses of up to 700 billion euros at their expense and undermines effective poverty reduction. What is regarded as a success story for liberalization by the IFIs, is regarded in this way from the perspective of the development programme of the United Nations: 'these institutions rely with their economic–political suggestions and their political conditionality on a narrowed view of the world, which reflects the interests of its most powerful members'.

This is one of the points that challenge the credibility of the overall policy of IFIs. Without addressing this macroeconomic dimension, the practical programmes and projects within the Millennium Goals cannot succeed; instead, they tend to become a sort of alibi rather than paths of hope.

Here are some fundamental questions about the policy of the IMF and the World Bank:

1 Does the World Bank really think that the international financial markets are basically fully operative, so that shortcomings have only to be discussed as improvements in the field of so-called microeconomic governance?

2 Does the World Bank view shortcomings as primarily located in the developing countries rather than the industrialized countries?

3 Does the World Bank largely reject macroeconomic governance measures?

4 Does the World Bank still assume that the entire world is to take its bearings from the financial markets, reformed in this way, as quickly as possible?

5 Does the World Bank still assume that international financial institutions are to remain virtually unchanged?

I assume and hope that the answer to these questions will be five times 'no'.

Neither is it enough to be dedicated to the Millennium Development Goals, important as they are. At first glance, it seems as if we could become allies, with different roles but the same goals. However, whether or not we are able to define this kind of complementary approach may depend on the following questions:

- Do you see the World Bank in the meantime as aiming at a 'justice of results'? If so, what are the indicators?

- Does the World Bank see common ground with churches that are committed to 'justice for the poorest of the poor'?

I close with some questions for possible further discussion:

- Do you agree that the problems are not confined to developing countries, but also exist in the institutions of industrialized countries? If not, why not? If so, what are the implications? Where do you see the responsibility of industrialized countries for developing countries?

- What are the necessary means of macro-governance within the present financial order, if there are any?

- What guiding principles apply to the speed of reforms and what measures have to be taken concerning industrialized and developing countries?

- What need do you see for reform of international organizations like the IMF and World Bank? Should developing countries simply and solely have better access to these institutions, or is more radical reform necessary, such as a shift in decision-making powers within the IMF and World Bank in favour of developing countries, and new sets of defined tasks for the IFIs? Can you imagine a new, strong IMF and World Bank, focused on fighting poverty in the context of justice and the option for the poor?

Many questions, I know. And if we are all truly committed to a holistic understanding of sustainable development, there is yet another question: in what ways does the World Bank require our assistance as churches to convert those within the organization (and its controlling organs) who at present prevent it from reforming in this way?

Notes

1   Martin Büscher and Lukas Menkhoff (2003), 'Gerechtigkeit und Effizienz – Optionen für eine gerechte internationale Finanzordnung. Zum Brückenbau zwischen wirtschaftsethischen Ansatzpunkten und finanzmarktpolitischen Instrumenten.' Zeitschrift für Evangelische Ethik (ZEE), 47. Jg. 2003, S. 210–22. The rest of this chapter is to a large extent based on their argumentation.
2   Ibid., p. 217.
3   Ibid., p. 218.

7

Wealth Creation and Social Justice

Flemming Larsen

It is not an easy task to convince critics of the International Monetary Fund that the IMF's views and actions are driven by ethical considerations and concern for people's welfare. When they think about the IMF, critics tend to associate concepts such as social injustice, austerity, violation of human rights, protection of the interests of financial speculators and transnational enterprises, and of course the dominance of US views. That we are often labelled neoliberal is clearly not meant as a tribute to a compassionate institution.

Before taking a closer look at our policies and actions, remember that the IMF emerged from the ashes of the Second World War as one of the cornerstones of a strong global economic system, based on cooperation, solidarity, the 'rule of law' in international economic relations, and mechanisms to help countries in financial distress. The objective was to help members achieve high living standards, and sustainable economic growth and development, while eschewing the beggar-thy-neighbour policies that had contributed to the Great Depression. The language of our Articles of Agreement, or the IMF's constitution, is somewhat technical, but there can be no doubt that ethical considerations were overarching among the IMF's founding fathers, who had all seen the devastating effects of the Great Depression and the two world wars.

Since then the Fund has evolved, and so has the language you will typically find in Fund policy statements. But the objectives of our work have not changed. If anything, our policy statements have become much more precise about the Fund's responsibility to guide member countries on some – but certainly not all – of the essential prerequisites for economic progress, namely macroeconomic and financial stability. This is because economic and financial stability has proven again and again to be an absolutely necessary condition for sustained improvements in living standards, especially as economic and financial instability and crises are almost always felt disproportionately by the poor. In addition, with respect to the Fund's important but less than all-encompassing responsibilities, it is because the membership considers that the Fund is most effective when it concentrates on the core issues that form its mandate.

Safeguarding macroeconomic and financial stability, and restoring it as rapidly as possible after economic crises, are clearly the dominant concerns of the Fund. We in the Fund consider that by fulfilling these responsibilities we are contributing to a better world. We also consider that we are contributing in a major way to protecting those who are the most vulnerable, to reducing poverty, and to enhancing social justice – within countries and across the world. We also help to protect the vulnerable and reduce poverty through advice on the allocation of public spending and the design of social safety nets. While we do not usually frame our objectives in terms of human rights, in my view the IMF's work clearly is geared toward protecting what I consider basic human rights: the right to work, save, invest, engage in enterprise, and secure the future of one's family in a reasonably predictable economic and financial environment characterized by low and stable inflation, respect for property rights, and the right to compete without discrimination based on race, religion or country of birth.

It is true of course that there is not a single bridge, road, school or hospital to point to as something that the IMF has financed. What we can point to as a success is when a country manages to reduce an unsustainable fiscal deficit and therefore avoids a fiscal crisis. Or when a country rapidly tackles the root causes of a financial crisis and thereby can emerge from a recession relatively quickly and resume solid economic growth. Even in cases such as these, what we will be remembered for, and blamed for, is typically the fiscal belt-tightening or structural adjustments we are perceived to have 'imposed' as a condition for financial assistance. And it does sometimes happen that the government of a country we have assisted is happy to join the chorus of blame for the 'harsh' measures that had to be adopted – overlooking conveniently that it was the government's own policy mistakes or mismanagement that may have contributed importantly to the crisis in the first place.

This is indeed our key public relations challenge: we find it hard sometimes to get across that the work of the IMF represents a cooperative effort by the world community to assist countries in difficulty; that we provide this assistance through the best possible advice our professional knowledge and experience suggest is appropriate in a given case, together with short-term financial assistance at much easier terms than the market would provide in a crisis; that our efforts thereby allow the crisis-struck country to recover much faster, and at much lower economic and social costs, than if it had to act on its own. For all of that the IMF is seldom given credit.

Critics are also happy to point to the IMF's mistakes. In Argentina, for example, a recent article in Le Figaro essentially blamed the IMF for misguided advice throughout the 1990s that eventually led to the crisis, then for failing to prevent the financial meltdown that followed, and finally for failing to come up with quick solutions to restore economic growth and external creditworthiness. What about the role of the authorities, the mistakes made by domestic and foreign investors, and the impact of external shocks? Nobody else appears to have had anything to do with Argentina's problems, whereas it seems our lot to be the world's scapegoat of first resort.

Not that we do not make mistakes. We did not sufficiently warn emerging market countries in the 1980s and early 1990s about the requirements for a successful liberalization of short-term capital flows; and we underestimated the fragility of financial systems in some countries – partly because information about the levels of non-performing loans that had been accumulating in the booms preceding the crises was only revealed – reluctantly – by the authorities after the panics had started. We have the capacity to recognize that we have made mistakes, to take into account differences among countries, and to suggest alternative policies, based on a constant effort of research and evaluation. The image of the Fund as a static, dogmatic bureaucracy that always prescribes the same medicine to everybody is totally wrong.

The IMF is also criticized for what is viewed as our unreserved promotion of globalization. We look at globalization as a trend propelled by technological progress and the desires of consumers, workers and holders of financial assets, and with predominantly (though not solely) positive consequences. There is strong evidence, for example, that trade liberalization can be a powerful driving force for economic development, but that the process of liberalization involves adjustment costs for some groups that countries need to deal with. There is nothing new in this: economic progress has always meant economic change with gainers as well as losers. As with other types of economic change, each country needs to face up to the challenges arising from globalization to maximize its benefits and minimize its adverse effects. And countries need to act together, cooperatively, to tackle those challenges that are common but beyond the capacity of any country to deal with on its own. The Fund sees itself as particularly well placed to advise members on some of the conditions necessary for a country to reduce its vulnerability to external shocks as a result of growing economic and financial integration. And we are of course also working with the entire membership to strengthen the global financial architecture, to make it less crisis prone, and to address abuses such as money laundering and financing of terrorism.

THE IMF'S ROLE IN LOW INCOME COUNTRIES
Some critics have gone so far as to call for the IMF to get out of Africa, to stop assisting (the critics would say to stop harming) the poorest countries. The fact is that these countries strongly disagree, as do virtually all of our member countries: they all see a vital role for the Fund in supporting our poorest members. Needless to say, IMF management and staff remain deeply committed to fulfilling this mandate.

It is important to be clear about the Fund's role, what we reasonably can be expected to accomplish and what lies beyond our mandate and competencies. Again, the principal areas in which we provide assistance to low-income countries are fiscal, monetary and exchange rate policies, the stability and soundness of the financial system, and macroeconomic governance and institutions – through policy advice, technical assistance, capacity building and concessional financial assistance.

In recent years, the World Bank and the IMF have jointly been helping countries develop a framework to make choices about their development strategies, as formulated in the Poverty Reduction Strategy Paper (PRSP). The IMF's principal role is to help ensure that the PRSP is consistent with macroeconomic and financial stability to help justify the Fund's own financial support and also help mobilize financial support from the broader international community. We also offer technical assistance to help establish and strengthen policy-making institutions, in particular to translate medium-term development priorities and action plans into budget allocations and to help establish systems to track execution of expenditures in priority sectors. For the most heavily indebted countries, the IMF and the World Bank are helping to reduce external debt burdens in a durable way through the HIPC initiative; this initiative has already helped to increase the share of public expenditures that can be allocated to education, health spending, and other policies that benefit the poor. But it is not the IMF's business to intervene in defining countries' development strategies. That is beyond our mandate and our competencies. Instead, this task is up to each country in cooperation with its development partners (especially the World Bank) and domestic stakeholders such as the legislature, trade unions, business, religious groups and NGOs, including representatives of the poor. In this way, by fostering greater transparency around development strategy and openness in debate, the PRSP can help to empower advocates for the poor. In the most successful cases, the PRSP can thus become a framework for social cohesion.

There are in fact encouraging signs that many years' efforts to strengthen countries' macroeconomic foundations are beginning to pay off. In the countries that have pursued policies consistent with our advice, economic growth is generally up, inflation is increasingly under control, budget deficits have shrunk, and foreign exchange reserves have increased. All very good, you will probably say, but too little to make a sufficient difference, and far too little progress to allow the Millennium Development Goals, including deep reductions in poverty, to be achieved.

That is absolutely correct. Much more is needed to stimulate private sector development, raise living standards and improve the quality of life. Let me focus on one particular dimension: wealth creation and social justice.

Wealth creation is at the heart of economic development. Without wealth creation there can be no development, no growth in the tax base and therefore in social expenditures, and no social justice. To accelerate wealth creation requires high rates of investment in physical and human capital and increased efficiency in the production process. Let me start with human capital, where the prevalence of diseases such as malaria and HIV/AIDS and inadequate education not only represent formidable challenges to improving the human condition, but also have severe consequences by limiting production capacity. Most PRSPs rightly try to address the severe shortcomings in the supply of public goods and human capital protection and formation. The IMF supports this emphasis by helping countries design their budgets with the objective of increasing the share of public resources allocated to poverty-reducing programmes. The World Bank and the IMF are also helping countries strengthen their public expenditure management, in order to make sure that budgeted resources do in fact reach intended recipients.

Physical capital formation represents an equally formidable challenge. Only countries able to stimulate domestic private sector savings and investment and entrepreneurship will achieve the rates of growth in output and employment needed to achieve the Millennium Development Goals. Even substantial amounts of foreign aid and investment cannot have a lasting effect in the absence of greater private sector dynamism. For this, it should not surprise you that a representative of the IMF will insist that macroeconomic stability is a sine qua non. But so are political stability, an absence of corruption, a growth-friendly regulatory and institutional environment, respect for property rights, and a stable, efficient financial system that can channel countries' financial resources toward productive investment projects. Much remains to be done in these areas across most of the developing world and the economies in transition from central planning. It is encouraging that many PRSPs are being used to start addressing governance problems. The Fund's role in this area is mainly to help build capacity and strengthen countries' institutions. In Africa, for example, we have recently established two technical assistance centres to better coordinate and target the considerable amount of technical assistance the Fund is providing in the areas of our core competencies, often with the help of funds and experts made available by advanced member countries.

In the Fund, with our traditional focus on (you might say, obsession with) sustainability, we are also paying a great deal of attention to the fact that many low-income countries remain highly vulnerable to natural disasters and external shocks beyond their control, including falling commodity prices. In too many cases, the progress a country has been making can be reversed almost overnight. Much of our advice therefore is geared toward helping countries strengthen their resilience, including the provision of temporary financial assistance to help in the country's adjustment effort. These efforts very much benefit the poor, since poverty often increases during periods of economic instability.

The Fund's financial assistance to low-income countries is in the form of adjustment financing, typically at concessional terms and with a longer reimbursement period than for middle- and high-income members. Such adjustment financing helps countries stabilize after crises and assists them when they need to adjust their policies to strengthen their fundamentals and hence their growth potential. The Fund also provides financial assistance to countries experiencing temporary export shortfalls or increased import bills for cereals, or facing urgent balance of payments needs in the wake of natural disasters or armed conflicts. In addition, the executive board is currently considering providing assistance to countries that may face temporary adjustment costs as a result of meeting obligations under the Doha round. However, all of the Fund's assistance is temporary and cannot serve as long-term development finance; this needs to come from bilateral donors and multilateral development banks. Eventually, and hopefully in the foreseeable future, as some low-income countries reach a more mature stage and establish a record of consistent policy formulation and execution, foreign direct investment and other types of private capital flows are expected to begin to supplement, and eventually replace, such official flows.

Finally, I want to mention the Fund's advocacy role. We are working closely with the official aid community to encourage debt forgiveness for highly indebted low-income countries. We are also working to promote higher aid levels, grants instead of loans, untied assistance rather than tied to specific purchases, harmonization of donor practices to reduce the burden for recipient countries, and greater aid predictability. To illustrate how the Fund liaises with donors, I can mention that one of my staff in Paris is a permanent observer to the OECD's Development Assistance Committee. We also remain a strong critic of the industrial countries' agricultural policies and an unwavering proponent for the developing countries' interests in the Doha trade round. There is no better illustration of the IMF's views in this area than the statement issued last week by our Managing Director together with the heads of the World Bank and the OECD.

DECLARATION BY THE HEADS OF THE IMF, OECD AND WORLD BANK

Next week, trade ministers will gather at Cancún to advance the Doha Development Agenda. They carry with them the aspirations of millions around the world whose hopes for economic advancement rest on opportunities in the global economy. Trade is a driving force for economic expansion in developed and developing countries alike. Promoting the growth of trade is essential for global economic prosperity. And the Doha negotiations are a central pillar of the global strategy to achieve the Millennium Development Goals: a strategy to reduce poverty by giving poor people the opportunity to help themselves.

Ambitions for Cancún must be commensurate with these objectives. We need a decisive break with trade policies that hurt economic development. Donors cannot provide aid to create development opportunities with one hand and then use trade restrictions to take these opportunities away with the other – and expect that their development dollars will be effective. Developing countries have an important responsibility in using the multilateral system to promote better integration among themselves and with the global economy. Their tariffs and non-tariff barriers stand as major obstacles to their mutual trade.

All countries have an interest in a successful outcome – and all have a duty to promote a broad and balanced agenda. But appropriate action by the developed countries is crucial. In this regard, we applaud the progress that has been made in negotiating public health exceptions under the TRIPS Agreement and encourage the parties at Cancún to build on the recent momentum in the talks on agriculture.

Agriculture is of particular importance to the economic prospects of many developing countries, and reforming the current practices in global farm trade holds perhaps the most immediate scope for bettering the livelihoods of the world's poor. Yet developed countries impose tariffs on agriculture that are 8 to 10 times higher than on industrial goods. Many continue to use various forms of export subsidies that drive down world prices and take markets away from farmers in poorer countries. In every sector except agriculture, these same countries long ago agreed to prohibit export subsidies. Agricultural support costs the average household in the EU, Japan and United States more than a thousand US dollars a year. Much of this support depresses rural incomes in developing countries while benefiting primarily the wealthiest farmers in rich countries, and does little to accomplish the environmental and rural community goals that developed countries strive to pursue.

Trade can be a powerful tool for development. To be fully effective, trade policy should be placed firmly within national strategies for development and poverty reduction, and be built on a foundation of good governance. Realizing the benefits of greater trade will require complementary efforts. On the supply side, this means investments in infrastructure necessary to ensure that the products of the poor can reach global markets and, in the longer run, investments in education. And it means policies to safeguard the interests of the most vulnerable in society. Both often require external technical and financial assistance. We are ready to help. All our organizations have stepped up efforts to provide 'aid for trade' in support of a positive outcome of the Doha talks. Together, we have the mandates, the resources and the expertise to assist countries in managing the adjustment pressures that can be associated with more open trade.

But the key challenges now lie with governments. All have to do their part. Rich countries have to take the lead in areas now blocking the talks, particularly agriculture. Middle-income countries have to contribute as well, reducing tariffs that affect not only their own citizens but also other developing countries. And low-income countries, even as they receive more aid for trade and win more time to implement some WTO rules, have to assume new responsibilities of participation in the international system.

Working together the international community has an opportunity to help the world's poor. We should not let it slip away.

8

Response to IMF

Atle Sommerfeldt

It may be an overstatement to say that the WCC, World Bank and IMF are born of the same roots, as was claimed by the representative of the IMF. However, it is true that all three organizations were born in the aftermath of the Second World War and were faced with the challenge of building a new world order, to reconstruct countries, communities and economies destroyed by war. The same governments that established the World Bank and the IMF also established international human rights institutions, starting with the Universal Declaration on Human Rights. This international human rights system is key to our performance in three major areas of concern:

1   It provides the paradigm for understanding the purpose of economic growth: to create the possibility for fulfilling the human rights of all people. To achieve this, economic growth is certainly necessary, but certainly not sufficient. The human rights paradigm is also better than most of our own attempts in the ecumenical movement to establish the criteria for economic life, which we hardly agree upon ourselves and which are far from universal recognition.

2   It provides the criteria for measuring results, be it macroeconomic policies or development programmes. The problem with the IFIs is not (as is claimed by some of us in the ecumenical movement) that they place too much emphasis on efficiency and results. The problem is that they have not been efficient enough and sufficiently results oriented to achieve the overarching objective set by the governments that established them: all human rights for all people.

3   Through the institutional mechanisms of the human rights system, we also have an established space for accountability for the IFIs, and civil society and market actors as well. The present work in the Human Rights Commission on the effects of SAPs is an indication that this is not only theory.

I agree that the labelling of the World Bank and IMF as neoliberal institutions is neither accurate nor very fruitful, for it drives the ecumenical movement into endless discussions about ideology, abstractions and concepts. I find it much more useful to argue in terms of markets, states and civil society, all of which are necessary to achieve the goal of all human rights for all people. The balance between the three is the proper agenda for debate, and the correct balance has to be contextual, both in space and time. When it is claimed as a matter of ideology that any one of these formations represents the final solution – be it market forces, government or civil society – then we have to respond critically. As important as it has been to unmask faith in the market as the solution, we also have to criticize Marxist political economy and one-sided government-run development. Sometimes, when I read ecumenical documents, I have the feeling that we think government is the solution or that local communities are sufficient. However, I do support the view that we need to challenge the inherent positivistic basis in most schools of economics, including neoliberal and Marxist political economy.

THE IMF

I agree with Professor Söderbaum: we have to work according to an arena–actor–agenda matrix. My first point here is that IFIs must be seen as arenas and therefore any purely ideological critique of them is not very fruitful. They are set up as instruments for governments and are therefore arenas for actors with different agendas. Instead of discussing the arena, we should concentrate on the actors with agendas in the arena and talk of organizations as actors with agendas.

The IMF as an arena was set up by governments with a specific agenda. The problem, however, is that governments have delegated most of the policy making to central banks and finance ministries. Political accountability is weak. The ecumenical movement has to take some responsibility for this, as we have not been vigorous enough (at least not in Norway) to make a nation's performance in the IMF a normal part of political debate. The issue of governance is also important: the IMF is not a model for democracy and transparency in decision making.

The IMF as an actor is no longer a strong player in the globalized economy. It has very limited powers compared with the main players – the OECD countries and transnational corporations. Following what is generally accepted as the poor performance of the IMF in the Asia crisis, the establishment of alternative institutions in East Asia is being discussed. The failure of neoclassical economics and liberalization as the solution to crises is also demonstrated in Russia. This means that the IMF is significantly weakened as an actor and that its agenda is not very clear. The main area in which it is still a major actor concerns countries struggling with poverty and debt. This may be the reason why the IMF has put poverty eradication higher on the agenda, as the only legitimate way of dealing with countries in the poverty trap is to deal with poverty itself. Part of its mandate, which has been sleeping for decades, is therefore revitalized. The problem, however, is the IMF's inadequate institutional capacity and competence for dealing with poverty.

My main problem with the IMF is its lack of responsibility. The IMF gives advice, pushes structural adjustments, gives loans. Some of the advice and some of the policies may work, but most of them have not, at least as measured by their ability to promote human rights for all people. The IMF does not take responsibility for its mistakes, nor for the consequences of those mistakes. As ecumenical actors 'on the ground' in most countries involved with the IMF, we meet and work with those people who suffer the consequences of its failed policies. The costs of those failed policies are not met by the IMF, nor by those who mismanaged in government or the private sector, but by ordinary people. This is the main moral and ethical problem with the IMF. Commentators and witnesses who should know (e.g. Joseph Stiglitz) claim that the cultural view in the IMF is that human suffering is a price we have to pay. This is a Pol Pot way of arguing and can only be upheld as long as the IMF does not take responsibility for – face the consequences of – its failed policies. The most immediately obvious of these failures is the debt crisis and the refusal to take responsibility for illegitimate or odious debt.

Conclusion
The IMF must find a way of taking responsibility for its actions. This should be the main moral and ethical agenda for us in the ecumenical movement, which will allow us to tackle more specific issues, the most important of which is the issue of illegitimate debt.

9

The International Concept of Wealth Creation and Social Justice: A WCC Perspective

Pamela K. Brubaker

> The fundamental tenets of the current development model – 'progress, pro-
> ductivity, profits' – has brought with it the dispossession of the majority of
> the people, the desacralizing of nature, the destruction of the way of life of
> entire cultures, and the degradation of women.
> Corinne Kumar-D'souza (Gnanadason, Kanyoro and McSpadden, 1996)

Although the WCC, the World Bank and the IMF share the common objective of poverty eradication based on values and ethics of life,

> the ecumenical community expressly rejects the neoliberal economic poli-
> cies promoted by the World Bank and the IMF … Far from reducing pover-
> ty or enhancing ecological sustainability, these policies have widened the
> gap between the wealthy and the poor, and have resulted in greater social
> exclusion and greater exploitation of the earth's resources … By asserting
> justice, ecological sustainability and the creation of viable communities as
> our goals, the ecumenical community's emphasis differs from the dominant
> approach, which focuses on fostering economic growth … For the ecumeni-
> cal community, authentic human development can never be achieved when
> the ultimate goal is the amassing of wealth and material goods, creating an
> unquenchable thirst for more power, profits, and possessions.

These excerpts from the WCC paper 'Justice: The Heart of the Matter' succinctly describe the views of the ecumenical community on wealth creation and social justice. In this chapter, I will elaborate the ecumenical critique of the neoliberal market ideology that informs the policies and practices of the international finan-cial institutions, and explore the ecumenical vision of just, sustainable communi-ties, concluding with a discussion of pressing challenges.

ECUMENICAL CRITIQUE

The WCC has clearly and repeatedly stated in different venues that it rejects the neoliberal economic policies promoted by the World Bank and IMF.[1] The harmful effects of the Washington consensus – liberalization, deregulation and privatiza-tion – on the world's people – particularly the poor – and the earth itself are well documented. This form of economic globalization has led to increased inequality and environmental degradation. A study by Mattias Lundberg and Lyn Squire of the World Bank found that 'the poor are far more vulnerable to shifts in relative international prices, and this vulnerability is magnified by the country's openness to trade … at least in the short term, globalization appears to increase both pover-ty and inequality' (cited in Bello, 2001: 239–40).

Activist Shalmali Guttal concluded in her study of globalization in Asia that biodiversity and environmental quality are threatened by export-oriented economic growth, which takes place through 'commercial harvesting of natural resources for value added production and an increase in plantation and mono-cropping'. Privatization of land, water and resource rights are also a factor. These processes also alienate local communities, many of which are indigenous, from the common resource base they depend upon. A report on neoliberal economic restructuring in ten African countries found that 'all too often policy decisions reinforce or aggravate existing inequalities ... in many cases, economic restructuring has increased poverty and further marginalized women' (Brubaker, 2001: 39).

The US Congress' Advisory Commission on International Financial Institutions, also known as the Meltzer Commission, supported many of the claims made by critics of the IMF and World Bank. Its report, issued early in 2000, concluded (1) instead of promoting economic growth, the IMF institutionalizes economic stagnation; (2) the World Bank is irrelevant rather than central to the goal of eliminating poverty (Bello, 2001: 60).

The Meltzer Commission came up with a number of devastating findings: '70 per cent of the Bank's non-grant lending is concentrated in 11 countries, with 145 other member countries left to scramble for the remaining 30 per cent; 80 per cent of the Bank's resources are devoted not to the poorest developing countries but to the better off ones with positive credit ratings ... the failure rate of bank projects is 65–70 per cent in the poorest countries and 55–60 per cent in all developing countries (Bello, 2001: 240–1).

Former World Bank Chief Economist Joseph Stiglitz has published articles and a book criticizing the policies of the IMF. He is particularly critical of the deregulation of capital markets, claiming it increases risk without increasing growth (Stiglitz, 2000). In Globalization and Its Discontents (2002) Stiglitz charges: 'Ideology guided policy prescriptions and countries were expected to follow the IMF guidelines without debate.' Not only did these policies often produce poor results, but also 'they were antidemocratic'. Furthermore, 'those policies weren't questioned by many of the people in power in the IMF' (Stiglitz, 2002: xiv).

These failures led both the World Bank and the IMF to declare a change in their policies, in order to focus on both economic growth and poverty reduction. According to a 1999 statement from the Group of Seven finance ministers and Central Bank governors, a 'comprehensive development framework' replaced existing structural adjustment programmes. This new paradigm included the following elements (reported in Bello, 2001: 50–1):

- Increased and more effective fiscal expenditures for poverty reduction with better targeting of budgetary resources, especially on social priorities in basic education and health.
- Enhanced transparency, including monitoring and quality control over fiscal expenditures.
- Stronger country ownership of the reform and poverty reduction process and programmes, involving public participation.
- Stronger performance indicators that can be monitored for follow-through on poverty reduction.

At this time, the IMF established the Poverty Reduction and Growth Facility, which replaced the Enhanced Structural Adjustment Programmes. Any programmes supported by the PRGF are 'framed around comprehensive, country owned Poverty Reduction Strategy Papers'. The IMF and World Bank cooperate in this endeavour, particularly on issues of conditionality.

The ecumenical community is not persuaded that these recent poverty eradication initiatives of the World Bank and IMF – although perhaps more in line with the human development consensus of growth with equity[2] – adequately break with neoliberal ideology; thus, it doubts their potential effectiveness. For instance, Jubilee 2000/USA (a broad coalition of religious and human rights groups) reviewed the Poverty Reduction Strategy Paper process and concluded: 'the injustice that macroeconomic reform conditions have not been subordinated to poverty reduction concerns is most disturbing'.

An examination of some recent IMF and World Bank documents and reports supports this charge. The IMF/World Bank PRSP Sourcebook states the 'principles of the Comprehensive Development Framework':

> The objective is to encourage low-income countries to reduce poverty by focusing on a renewed growth-oriented strategy ... Economic growth is the single most important factor influencing poverty, and macroeconomic stability is essential for high and sustainable rates of growth. Hence, macroeconomic stability should be a key component of any poverty reduction strategy ... In most cases, sustained high rates of growth also depend upon key structural measures, such as regulatory reform, privatization, civil service reform, improved governance, trade liberalization, and banking sector reform.

The IMF executive board review of the Poverty Reduction and Growth Facility[3] in March of 2002 reported: 'Directors saw an increased focus on the sources of growth in the PRGF-supported programmes as being of particular importance'. They stressed the importance of incorporating structural reforms to develop the private sector, increase foreign direct investment, enhance external competitiveness and increase labour productivity. The World Bank executive board approved a Private Sector Development Strategy (PSDS) in February 2002. The PSDS states: 'A significant part of the [World Bank Group's] existing work on policy reforms, such as that on privatization, competition policy, deregulation and strengthening of property rights, will help improve the investment climate in client countries.' A key prong of the PSDS is to more systematically attach conditions to future loans that are meant to 'improve the investment climate' in developing countries.

Two recent decisions by the Fund indicate that this mandate is trumping commitment to poverty reduction and country ownership of their PRSP. According to Inter-Press Service, the IMF delayed Zambia's one billion dollars in debt relief until it sells its state-owned commercial bank. Nicaragua was told that it must privatize its vital water resources, despite legislation which would suspend any such plans without a national debate (Mekay, 2002).

In his evaluation of PRGF strategies, David Tannenbaum (2002: 9–10) notes: 'In the past, these reforms have translated into lower taxes on businesses that starve government of resources, labour law changes that weaken protections for workers, destabilized safety nets and lower wages'. The PSDS proposes subsidizing the lower-income groups who will be negatively impacted by these policies. Yet, as Tannenbaum notes, 'The WB's own Development Report 2000/2001 points out that subsidies often do not make it to their intended recipients because of "leakage" or capture of the subsidies by richer groups.'

> Developing country citizens' ability to affect these policies are constrained by the power dynamics between the Bank and borrowing countries – with poor countries willing to accept Bank-imposed conditions as a quid pro quo for Bank approval to obtain new loans to pay off old debts and maintain a credit rating … Although the Bank favours involvement in policy formation by organized labour and other citizen groups, 'that's up to the countries', says the spokesperson. 'One person's civil society is another person's terrorist group. In some countries, dealing with labour unions may be anathema, but listening to consumer groups may be appropriate.' (Tannenbaum, 2002: 11, 12)

Contrast this statement to the IDA and IMF document 'Good Practices for PRSP Design and Implementation', which states: 'The PRSP process is designed to be open and participatory and to include all major stakeholders, including CSOs (even those which may be out of favour with the government) ' (IDA and IMF, n.d.: 3).

A particularly disturbing example of privatization is IMF support for privatization of state-owned tobacco enterprises. The World Bank has identified tobacco use as an impediment to development. Its studies show 'that excise taxes work to reduce smoking rates and advance public health.' 'The Bank has also published important information on tobacco trade liberalization, finding that reduced tobacco tariffs and freer trade in tobacco products have dire consequences, raising smoking rates and increasing preventable death and disease.'

> The IMF has in many cases supported privatization of state-run tobacco companies, and has even supported reduction of tobacco excise taxes and tariffs – policies universally agreed among public health advocates to undermine public health goals. … The IMF push for tobacco privatization is unswerving, and appears to be part of its ideological commitment to privatization. In several cases, the IMF has pushed for privatization despite intense local opposition. (White and Weissman, 2002: 13)

The World Bank and IMF claim that many benefits accrue to developing countries from privatization and foreign direct investment. Technology transfer is one such benefit. In its paper 'Globalization: Threat or Opportunity?' IMF staff contend: 'Information exchange is an integral, often overlooked aspect of globalization. For instance, FDI brings not only expansion of the physical capital stock, but also technical innovation.' But as Stiglitz points out, the Uruguay Round of GATT strengthened intellectual property rights in an unbalanced way: 'It overwhelmingly reflected the interests and perspectives of the producers, as opposed to the users, whether in developed or developing countries' (Stiglitz, 2002: 8). Walden Bello observes that a crucial factor in the industrialization of most late-industrializing countries, including the US, is 'access to cutting-edge technology'. Yet this process of technological diffusion is now seen as piracy by industrial leaders. Since TRIPs take the side of the latter, it makes 'industrialization by diffusion much more difficult. UNCTAD charges that this is "a premature strengthening of the intellectual property system … that favours monopolistically controlled innovation over broad-based diffusion"' (Bello, 2001: 19–20). Similar critiques could be made of other claims about the benefits of economic globalization.[4]

The success of the IMF and World Bank's focus on poverty reduction is also questionable. The PRSP Sourcebook points out:

> Growth associated with progressive distributional changes will have a greater impact on poverty than growth which leaves distribution unchanged. Hence, policies which improve the distribution of income and assets within a society, such as land tenure reform, pro-poor public expenditure, and measures to increase the poor's access to financial markets, will also form essential elements of a country's poverty reduction strategy. ('Macroeconomic Issues', updated 1/23/03)

However, a Staff Report from February 2002 noted countervailing measures to lessen the negative impact of growth policies on the poor in PRGF-supported programmes 'are not always accompanied by PSIA [poverty and social impact analysis], and even where it exists, the scope and depth of PSIA varies considerably across programmes. Most notably, the majority of the PRGF-supported programmes with important social impacts are covered neither by PSIA nor countervailing measures' (IMF Staff, February 2002: 21). The Structural Adjustment Participatory Review International Network (SAPRIN) found that little of this analysis 'made its way into country programming or back to Washington; none made its way into the Bank's own adjustments assessments, much less into adjustment operations themselves' (SAPRIN, 2002: 2). This is in spite of the fact that Wolfensohn and the Bank, in engaging in SAPRI, 'had acknowledged the critical importance of consultation, local knowledge, experience and analysis to the formulation of economic policies'.

The crucial challenge from the ecumenical community is to the neoliberal understanding of wealth creation primarily as economic growth. We ask: Wealth for whom? At what price? In its report from the World Summit on Sustainable Development, the WCC states:

> The underlying development paradigm, with its strong emphasis on economic growth and market expansion, has served first and foremost the interests of powerful economic players. It has further marginalized the poor sectors of society, simultaneously undermining their basic security in terms of access to land, water, food, employment, other basic services and a healthy environment. (Echoes, 2002: 37)

Other analyses support these claims. For instance, a longitudinal study by independent researchers found that although there is some evidence that women's status overall tends to improve with economic development, economic growth can increase gender inequality (Forsythe, Korzeniewicz and Durant, 2000). A recent UNICEF study found 'there is no fixed relationship between the annual reduction rate of the U5MR and the annual rate of growth in per capita GDP' (UNICEF, 2002: 115).

The International Forum on Globalization starkly describes the vision that the embrace of 'unlimited expansion of trade and foreign investment' by the IMF and World Bank suggests:

> They consider the most advanced state of development to be one in which all productive assets are owned by foreign corporations producing for export; the currency that facilitates day-to-day transactions is borrowed from foreign banks; education and health services are operated by foreign corporations on a for-profit, fee-for-service basis; and almost everything that local people consume is imported.

Clearly, such policies 'consolidate and serve the wealth and power of a small corporate elite' (IFG, 2002: 52).

IFG member Walden Bello contends 'both institutions [IMF and World Bank] are to a great extent driven by the interests of key political and economic institutions in the Group of Seven countries – particularly in the case of the IMF, the US government and US financial interests' (Bello, 2001: 60). Joseph Stiglitz makes similar claims about the IMF, also noting the cost of these policies: 'Inside the IMF it was simply assumed that whatever suffering occurred was a necessary part of the pain countries had to experience on the way to becoming a successful market economy, and that their measures would, in fact, reduce the pain the countries would have to face in the long run.' Although Stiglitz thinks 'some pain was necessary', in his judgment 'the level of pain in developing countries created in the process of globalization and development as it has been guided by the IMF and international economic organizations has been far greater than necessary' (Stiglitz, 2002: xiv).

ECUMENICAL VISION

The philosophy and vision of the ecumenical community differ radically from that of institutions which focus on fostering economic growth. 'For the ecumenical community, authentic human development can never be achieved when the ultimate goal is the amassing of wealth and material goods, creating an unquenchable thirst for more power, profits and possessions' (WCC, Justice). In place of unlimited economic growth, we envision sustainable human development based on a just, moral and caring economy. We believe equity and human rights are central to poverty eradication; poverty is not just lack of monetary resources. Our vision is of a world filled with just, sustainable communities.

The WCC challenges the underlying anthropology of neoliberal economic globalization, which 'views humans as individuals rather than as persons in community, human beings as essentially competitive rather than cooperative, and human beings as materialist at the exclusion of the spiritual'. Furthermore, 'economic globalization also threatens the diversity of cultures.' (WCC Central Committee, 2001.) Instead, the ecumenical community offers 'an alternative way of life of community in diversity' grounded in a life-centred vision that affirms God's gift of life to all creation. Four essentials of this vision are to be nurtured:

1   Participation: the optimal inclusion of all at every level.
2   Equity: basic fairness that extends to all life forms.

3 Accountability: 'the structuring of responsibility toward one another and the earth itself.'

4 Sufficiency: a commitment to meet the basic needs of all life possible and to develop 'a quality of life that includes bread for all but is more than bread alone'. (WCC, 1998: 23)

This vision shares much with the people-centred consensus developed by the network of groups protesting against corporate- and finance-ruled globalization. The International Forum on Globalization claims 'the foundation of all real wealth' is 'common heritage resources'. These resources 'constitute a collective birthright of the whole species to be shared equitably among all'. It identifies three categories of common heritage resources:

> The first category includes the water, land, air, forests and fisheries on which everyone's life depends. The second includes the culture and knowledge that are collective creations of our species. Finally, more modern common resources are those public services that governments perform on behalf of all peoples to address such basic needs as public health, education, public safety, and social security, among others.

All these resources 'are under tremendous strain as corporations seek to privatize and commodify them' (IFG, 2002: 63–4).

For the WCC, a key policy objective is to finance, develop, manage and conserve these resources as 'global public goods'. Other key policies include promotion of just trade, regulation of financial markets to control speculation, and people-centred financing for development. Both the WCC and the IFG have detailed discussions of policies for a people-centred globalization, as well as examples of places where these policies have worked.

The possibilities and limitations of income generation policies and programmes for low-income people deserve critical scrutiny, as they have been supported by the IFIs and the WCC. Since the success of the Grameen Bank in Bangladesh in making small loans to poor women who used them to build income-generating projects that substantially improved their families' well-being, micro-credit programmes are viewed by some as the solution to poverty. Grameen Bank founder Muhammad Yunus cautions that experience shows that unless the poorest of the poor are specifically targeted by these programmes, 'they will be excluded as they are from almost every other opportunity'. He further cautions that micro-credit alone will not empower the poor or lead to any significant drop in absolute poverty; other programmes, like girls' education and youth employment opportunities, are also necessary. These points resonate with the 'human capabilities' approach to development articulated by Amartya Sen and Martha Nussbaum, who argue 'poverty can be sensibly identified in terms of capability deprivation; the approach concentrates on deprivations that are intrinsically important (unlike low income, which is only instrumentally significant)' (Sen, 1999: 87).

Income generating projects can also increase the workload of women, which may already have intensified during periods of economic restructuring when crises in social reproduction are exacerbated. Economist Diane Elson argues that the intensification and extension of unpaid labour – what sociologist Saskia

Sassen calls 'the feminization of survival' – is a hidden factor in many episodes of stabilization and structural adjustment. Unpaid labour can help absorb the shocks of adjustment, since it replaces paid labour in the production of daily necessities such as food and clothing. In her study of projects in Nepal, economist Katharine Rankin discovered that without the development of a collective consciousness of subordination, income generating projects can perpetuate 'oppressive relations'. She contends: 'Micro finance demonstrates a clear gender dimension to this governmental function: here the transition from state-led to market-led approaches to poverty alleviation has been anchored to women's capacity to leverage social capital on behalf of the financial sustainability of formal lending institutions' (Rankin, 2002: 17–18).

Another crisis in social reproduction is the 'globalization of mothering' – or global care chains – which arises in part from the 'care deficit' that has emerged in the wealthier countries as women enter the workforce, which pulls migrants from the Third World and post-communist nations to become care-givers, while poverty pushes them. In their introduction to Global Woman (2003), Barbara Ehrenreich and Arlie Hochschild argue: 'This trend toward global redivision of women's traditional work throws new light on the entire process of globalization'. It suggests 'a dependency of a particularly intimate kind … as affluent and middle-class families in the First World come to depend on migrants from poorer regions to provide child care, homemaking and sexual services.' This global relationship

> in some way mirrors the traditional relationship between the sexes. The First World takes on a role like that of the old-fashioned male in the family – pampered, entitled, unable to cook, clean, or find his socks. Poor countries take on a role like that of the traditional woman within the family – patient, nurturing and self-denying. This sexual division of labour feminists[5] critiqued when it was 'local' has now gone global, with the inevitable trauma of children left behind. (Ehrenreich and Hochschild, 2003: 11–13)

The ecumenical community insists that debt forgiveness is essential to poverty eradication and building sustainable community. The WCC is very critical of debt relief programmes like HPIC, which are a means to achieve debt sustainability, not poverty eradication. Of particular concern is the new condition of HPIC-II that countries produce PRSPs. When I first learned about this, it brought to mind economist Mark Weisbrot's charge that the heart of the problem is 'the dominant globalizing institutions are continuously altering the rules of the game so as to redistribute income and power upward'. Although the expressed concern of HPIC-II is to ensure that funds made available through debt relief go toward poverty reduction, the overall intent is to ensure that the loans are repaid. This benefits the corporate and financial elite at the expense of the world's many poor people. It inhibits any real redistribution of wealth.

The ecumenical community demands debt forgiveness for highly indebted poor countries and debt restructuring for middle-income indebted countries. We want 'a new just process of arbitration for international debt cancellation, one not dominated by creditors' (WCC, 1998). The basis for these proposals is the biblical Sabbath-jubilee tradition, which 'offers a critical mandate for periodically overcoming structural injustice and poverty and for restoring right relationships … The jubilee is a recognition that, left to its normal and uninterrupted course, power becomes more and more concentrated in a few hands, that without intervention every society slides into injustice.' This tradition provides a strong basis for both debt relief and land reform (WCC, 1998: 5.2, 8.4).

The IMF addresses some of these concerns in its proposal for a Sovereign Debt Restructuring Mechanism (SDRM). Overall, the proposed mechanism is rather limited and does not begin to address the real needs of heavily indebted countries. But what is most telling is the response to the question of why countries shouldn't be allowed to use the SDRM to disqualify 'odious' debt, such as debt related to arms purchases or debt accumulated by previous non-democratic or corrupt regimes. First, the IMF asserts, 'one of the key principles underlying the SDRM is that any interference with contractual relations should be limited to those measures that are necessary to resolve the most important collective action problems.' Notice that the concern is for those who are to collect the payments, not those who must pay no matter what the cost. The document then claims that 'disqualifying "odious" debt would involve a radical change in the validity of creditor claims and the sanctity of contracts, which would have adverse implications for the operation of capital markets' (IMF, January 2003: D10; emphasis added).

This is the closest the IMF comes to using moral or religious language, at least in the documents I have read. In response to the claim that some debts are 'odious' ('deserving hatred or repugnance'), the IMF speaks of the sanctity of contracts. Webster's Collegiate Dictionary gives two meanings for sanctity: '1: holiness of life and character. 2: a. the quality or state of being holy or sacred; b. pl sacred objects, obligations, or rights.' And to what does the IMF apply this term? Contracts. This claim certainly lends support to charges that neoliberal ideology 'is the new religion of the market'.

Here I think we come to the heart of the difference between the philosophies of the IMF – and perhaps the World Bank – and the ecumenical community. The international financial and trade institutions speak of property rights and the sanctity of contracts; the ecumenical community speaks of justice and human rights, the dignity of human life, and the sacredness of all creation. Now the IMF might also claim that it is concerned for justice, but it is in the most limited form – commutative justice – which pertains to contracts and is based in civil law, or the relations of members of society to each other. (Even at this point, there are those who challenge the justice of existing debt.) The ecumenical community is concerned about distributive justice, the community's distribution of benefits and burdens – the whole in relation to parts, as well as social justice – the common good of the community.

The IMF and those who oppose debt cancellation make much of what they call 'moral hazard' as a basis for their position. This is the argument that such action would encourage others unfairly to seek relief from their debts. George Soros charges: 'The current campaign against moral hazard is just an excuse for resisting any kind of interference with the market mechanism. This resistance is based on the false doctrine of our age, namely that financial markets automatically tend towards equilibrium' (Soros, 2000: 91). Soros argues instead for 'a level playing field'. The WCC elaborates on this idea of 'false doctrine' in describing the way 'the iron law of economics … assumes religious status, justifying massive exclusion and sacrifice of human lives and nature in the name of economic growth through privatization and the liberalized and deregulated market' (WCC, Temptation).

Although the IMF seems to find the notion of bankruptcy for a sovereign nation repugnant, Jeffrey D. Sachs notes that Adam Smith favourably mentioned bankruptcy for sovereign borrowers in The Wealth of Nations. In a paper for the Brookings Institute, Sachs observes that there are two motivations for bankruptcy laws: overcoming collective action problems and offering 'a fresh start' to insolvent debtors. The first is based on efficiency, the second both on efficiency and equity (Sachs, 2002: 1–2). Sachs contends:

> Any specific bankruptcy proposals launched in response to the IMF initiative should recognize the two intertwined motivations of bankruptcy: addressing the collective action problems and granting a fresh start … Repayments to creditors must be placed in the context of additional objectives: a fresh start for an insolvent sovereign, preservation of its public functions, and achievement of broad development objectives. (Sachs, 2002: 4–5)

Sachs is especially concerned about a fresh start for low-income countries, which 'have been stuck for two decades or more in a persistent debt trap from which they are not recovering'. For these countries, he suggests, 'the basic standard for debt collection should be to restructure debts in order to provide a macroeconomic framework within which the countries can achieve the Millennium Development Goals' (Sachs, 2002: 27). Research by the New Economics Foundation shows that countries in Africa will not be able to meet these goals without much greater debt relief than that scheduled under HPIC-II (Greenhill and Blackmore, 2002: 9).

CHALLENGES

Our efforts to build just, sustainable communities face two great challenges: (1) how to ensure that economic growth is guided by values of social justice; (2) how to correct the centrality of economic growth – particularly in the rich countries, which use a disproportionate and unfair share of the world's resources and contribute an excessive amount of pollution – so that global sustainability becomes reality.

In my judgement, these challenges are interrelated. Developing a process that prioritizes social justice will likely require the support of those powerful groups, particularly in the wealthy countries, whose 'lifestyles' are grossly inequitable. As David Hallman commented in the WCC's report on the World Summit on Sustainable Development: 'The countries and corporations which most benefit from the current economic model are also the ones that hold much of the power in international institutions such as at WSSD. They were not about to make commitments that would undermine their position of privilege and respond with urgency to global injustice and the ecological threats.'

The necessity of linking socioeconomic justice and ecological sustainability has been a recurring emphasis of the WCC (see, for example, Santa Ana, 1998; Goudzwaard and de Lange, 1995). Yet the churches, particularly in the North, have been slow to respond to this challenge. David Korten addresses the relationship between the environment and basic needs when he develops criteria for the use of the earth's resources: 'The appropriate concern is whether the available planetary resources are being used in ways that (1) meet the basic needs of all people, (2) maintain biodiversity, and (3) assure the sustained availability of comparable resource flows to future generations.' Ethicist Timothy Gorringe suggests: 'If the standard of living enjoyed by the North cannot be generalized, then the issue of consumption has to be addressed by the wealthy nations.' This is one of the most difficult challenges the ecumenical community faces.

Some Christians see this as not just a matter of ethics, but of faith itself: 'serve God or serve mammon'. Many thoughtful commentators believe that the ecological crisis cannot be approached just as a technical problem; it is also a spiritual problem.

> The WCC's perspective is grounded in its conviction about the sacred nature of all Creation, and about life as an interplay of spiritual and physical dimensions. We uphold the common human vocation to live in right relationship with our neighbours, the earth and the Creator, respecting the integrity of the earth and working for the health and well-being of all members of the earth community. Its sacred origin makes the earth the common inheritance of all peoples for all times, to be enjoyed in just, loving and responsible relationships with one another. (Echoes, 2002)

The WCC is holding regional consultations on economic globalization, which include representatives from other religions. They are finding common ground in a shared analysis and strategies for alternatives. These are some of the efforts to develop the political will crucial to meeting these challenges.

Recognition and protection of human rights (particularly the second generation of social, economic and cultural rights) are one important way of trying to ensure that social justice guides economic growth. Sol Picciotto, who holds the Chair in Law at the University of Lancaster, writes: 'Increasingly, proposals are being put forward to constitutionalize the global public sphere by the introduction of human rights principles. These aim to provide a counterweight to globalization based on the neoliberal dynamic of the removal of barriers and the unleashing of the forces of economic self-interest, by introducing obligations of respect for human values.' He notes that human rights have traditionally been obligations on states, whereas this is an effort to make human rights obligations on the activities of private actors, such as transnational corporations and international economic organizations (Picciotto, 2001: 339). At the conclusion of its 25th meeting, the UN Sub-Commission on Human Rights resolved that the World Bank and IMF are bound by obligations enshrined in United Nations Human Rights Covenants and must incorporate them into the formulation and review of PRSPs.

Participation and accountability (enforceable human rights) are essential, but will not be fully adequate if global power imbalances are not rectified. Financial resources are needed for poverty reduction and ecological sustainability. Walden Bello calls for an environmental Marshall Plan, with eco-friendly technology transfer (Bello, 2001: 175). The IMF, the World Bank and the ecumenical community call for rich countries to meet the UN target for development assistance of 0.7

per cent of GNP. The WCC and the movement for a people-centred globalization want this development fund to be controlled by the UN rather than the IFIs.

Conceptually, alternative ways of measuring value and well-being to growth in GDP could be useful in thinking about social justice and wealth creation. Such measures can help people rethink the meaning of wealth and poverty as being about more than money. Alternative measures can also have an impact on public policy and expenditures. Various people, such as Herman Daly and John Cobb, have developed alternative measures that are finding some use. Some are questioning the rules for what counts as consumption rather than investment. Jeffrey Sachs (2002: 9) comments on the irony, given what we know about development, that education and healthcare are considered consumption rather than investment.

The work of Marilyn Waring has been ground-breaking, particularly in relation to the value of women's unpaid labour. She also shows the irrationality of how value is assigned. For instance, she considers dung, which provides fertilizer, a source of cooking fuel, and in some countries a basic building material for use in construction, maintenance, and decoration. Dung is not included in a nation's livestock production accounts or energy production accounts. 'We also won't find the hours that women spend gathering, transporting, cooking with, processing, manufacturing or decorating with it recorded as work.' But in Nepal, the World Bank estimated that 8 million tons of dung are burned as fuel each year. As Waring says, this is a 'major instance of import substitution, and represents a national saving in terms of debt that would be incurred through the importation of commercial fuels if resourceful women had not processed the alternative' (IDRC, 1997).

Although assigning value to unpaid labour can be a useful strategy for making it visible and impacting policy to improve the welfare of unpaid labourers, it is not the only viable approach. A WCC consultation in Fiji reported:

> Subsistence economy is still important for the life of the people and merits much more attention and support compared to the destructive effects of the monetarized economy and the spirit of competition that accompanies it. One participant commented that 'people in the West understand that poor people are those who have no resources. But because our culture of communal sharing is so strong, for us the poor person is the one who has no family or friends.' (WCC, 'Island of Hope': 13, 18)

Another approach is the development of local currencies and systems of barter, which brings the process of wealth creation back into the community. Just, sustainable communities will have a plurality of economies. Although the challenges we face are great, the vision of a world with enough for all motivates the ecumenical community to deepen its critique of neoliberalism and to struggle together on the way to that world.

Notes

1   For example, at the UN Financing for Development Summit in March 2002 in Monterrey, Mexico, and the World Summit on Sustainable Development in Johannesburg, South Africa in September 2002.

2   'The ecumenical community rejects models of financing for development that simply increase monetary wealth without eradicating poverty, and

have no regard for how that wealth is generated or distributed. Models that focus on poverty reduction, long-term employment and environmental restoration contribute to growth as a by-product, not as an end in itself. In this respect, a "human development alternative", similar to that advocated by the UNDP, is much more in line with the goals of the ecumenical community' (WCC, Justice). 'Attacking poverty directly – as a matter of human rights, to accelerate development and to reduce inequality within and among nations – has become an urgent global priority' (UNFPA, 2003: 5).

3   This was a required two-year review of PRGF, scheduled when the initiative was adopted. The executive board claims growth is critical for achieving poverty reduction and attention to the sources of growth is essential in developing appropriate policies and projections. A factsheet on IMF conditionality also included 'price and trade liberalization' in a list of policies which 'address structural impediments to healthy growth' (from IMF Conditionality: A Factsheet, 4 December, 2002). This emphasis on growth is in part a response to a primary criticism that the IMF structural adjustment programmes caused economic stagnation.

4   For instance, Susan George points out that foreign direct investment 'consists mostly of mergers and acquisitions that result in harmful economic concentration and job losses, and in any case such investment flows to only a dozen or so countries' ('Another World Is Possible', Echoes, 21/2002: 9). For an exhaustive overview, see SAPRIN (2002).

5   Several major World Bank reports provide strong empirical evidence that the gender-based division of labour and the inequalities to which it gives rise tend to slow development, economic growth and poverty reduction. Gender inequalities often lower the productivity of labour, in both the short term and the long term, and create inefficiencies in labour allocation in households and the general economy. They also contribute to poverty and reduce human well-being.

References

Bello, Walden (2001). The Future In the Balance: Essays on Globalization and Resistance, Food First Books.

Brubaker, Pamela K. (2001). Globalization at What Price? Economic Change and Daily Life, Pilgrim Press.

Echoes: Justice, Peace and Creation News (21/2002). Special Issue on Global Economic Justice.

Ehrenreich, Barbara and Arlie Russell Hochschild (eds.) (2003). Global Woman: Nannies, Maids, and Sex Workers in the New Economy, Metropolitan Books.

Elson, Diane (1998). 'Talking to the Boys: Gender and Economic Growth Models.' In Feminist Visions of Development, Routledge, 155–70.

Forsythe, Nancy, Roberto Patricio Korzeniewicz and Valerie Durant (2000) 'Gender Inequalities and Economic Growth: A Longitudinal Evaluation.' Economic Development and Cultural Change 48, No. 3 (April): 573–617.

Gnanadason, Aruna, Musimbi Kanyoro and Lucia Ann McSpadden (eds.) (1996). Women, Violence, and Nonviolent Social Change, WCC..

Goudzwaard, Bob and Harry de Lange (1986). Beyond Poverty and Affluence: Toward an Economy of Care. WCC Publications and W. W. Eerdmans.

Greenhill, Romilly and Sasha Blackmore (2002). 'Relief Works: African Proposals for Debt Cancellation – and Why Debt Relief Works.' Report from Jubilee Research at the New Economics Foundation, August, http://www.jubileeresearch,org.

Hallman, David (n.d.). 'Report on the World Summit on Sustainable Development,' http://www.wcc-coe/org/wcc/what/jpc/wssd-report.html.

IDA and IMF (n.d.). 'Good Practices for PRSP Design and Implementation: A Summary for Practitioners,' 3.

Internationalization Forum on Globalization (2002). Alternatives to Economic Globalization: A Better World Is Possible, Berrett-Koehler Publishers.

IMF (2002). 'The Design of the Sovereign Debt Restructuring Mechanism – Further Considerations.' 27 November.

IMF (2003). 'Proposals for a Sovereign Debt Restructuring Mechanism (SDRM): A Factsheet.' January.

'IMF Board Discusses Possible Features of A Sovereign Debt Restructuring Mechanism' (2003). Public Information Notice (PIN) No. 03/06, 7 January 7.

IMF Staff (2002). 'Globalization: Threat or Opportunity?' Issue Brief 00/01, April 12, corrected January 2002.

IMF Staff (2002). 'Review of the Poverty Reduction and Growth Facility: Issues and Options.' February 14: 21.

International Development Research Centre (1997). 'IDRC Report.' Ottawa, 9 May.

Jubilee 2000/USA (2000). 'End of the Year Statement.'

Macan-Markar, Marwaan (2001). 'Labour-Rights: South Korea Leads in Putting Value in Women's Work.' Inter- Press Service, 25 October.

Mekay, Emad (2002). 'IMF Strong-Arming Debtors Despite New Lending Guidelines.' Inter-Press Service, 10 December.

North–South Institute (1999). 'Putting a Value on Unpaid Work.' North–South Institute Newsletter, Vol. E, No. 2.

Nussbaum, Martha (2000). Women and Human Development: The Capabilities Approach, Cambridge University Press.

Picciotto, Sol (2001). 'Democratizing Globalization.' In Daniel Drache (ed.), The Market or the Public Domain: Global Governance and the Asymmetry of Power, Routledge, 335–59.

Raddon, Mary-Beth (2002). 'Community Currencies, Value and Feminist Economic Transformation.' Women and Environments International Magazine, No. 54/55 (spring), 24–6.

Rankin, Katherine N. (2002). 'Social Capital, Microfinance, and the Politics of Development.' Journal of Feminist Economics, Vol. 8, No. 1, 1–24.

Sachs, Jeffrey D. (2002). 'Resolving the Debt Crisis of Low-Income Countries.' Brookings Papers on Economic Activity, 1.

Santa Ana, Julio (1998). Sustainability and Globalization, WCC Publications.

Sen, Amartya (1999). Development as Freedom, Alfred A. Knopf.

Soros, George (2000). 'The New Global Financial Architecture.' In Will Hutton and Anthony Giddens (eds), Global Capitalism, New Press, 86–92.

Stiglitz, Joseph E. (2002). Globalization and Its discontents, W. W. Norton.

Stiglitz, Joseph E. (2000). 'The Insider.' The New Republic, Vol. 222, No. 16–17 (17–24 April), 56–60.

Structural Adjustment Participatory Review International Network (SAPRIN) (2002). 'The Policy Roots of Economic Crisis and Poverty: A Multi-Country Assessment of Structural Adjustment.' April.

Tannenbaum, David (2002). 'Obsessed: The Latest Chapter in the World Bank's Privatization Plans.' Multinational Monitor, September, 9–12.

UNFPA (2003). State of World Population 2002, United Nations Publications.

UNICEF (2002). The State of the World's Children 2003, United Nations Publications.

Weisbrot, Mark (1999). Globalization, Centre for Economic and Policy Research.

White, Anna and Robert Weissman (2002). 'The Hand-Off to Big Tobacco: IMF Support for Privatization of State-Owned Tobacco Enterprises.' Multinational Monitor, September, 13–17.

World Bank (2002). Integrating Gender into the World Bank's Work, 2002. World Bank.

World Bank (2002). Overview of Poverty Reduction Strategies, last updated 11/21/2002. World Bank.

World Bank (2003). Poverty Reduction Strategy Sourcebook, World Bank, accessed 1/26/2003.

World Bank (n.d.). Private Sector Development Strategy – Directions for the World Bank Group, World Bank.

World Council of Churches (2001). 'The Island of Hope: An Alternative to Economic Globalization.' WCC.

World Council of Churches (2000). Justice: The Heart of the Matter: An Ecumenical Approach to Financing for Development. Paper prepared for the WCC by the Ecumenical Coalition for Economic Justice: A Project of Canadian Churches.

World Council of Churches (2001). 'Report of the Policy Reference Committee II (Adopted).' WCC Central Committee.

World Council of Churches (1998). Together on the Way. Report from the Eighth Assembly, Harare, Zimbabwe, December 1998, available at www.wcc-coe.org.

World Council of Churches (2002). Lead Us Not Into Temptation: Churches' Response to the Policies of International Financial Institutions, WCC.

World Council of Churches (2000). 'There Are Alternatives to Globalization.' WCC.

10

Institutional Mandates, Concepts of Development and the Commodification of Public Goods

Hellen Grace Akwii Wangusa

WATER: SOURCE OF LIFE

Water is considered as a sacred element in some religions and spiritualities. Is it ethical to privatize it?

Privatization, we were made to understand, is the sale of state-owned assets, but it also includes various kinds of divestitures of public duties to the private sector – a form of contracting out that introduces commercial principles and reduces a government's role in providing goods and services. Besides lowering government expenditures, privatization is seen as a valid and effective means of rescuing non-performing public assets, ensuring efficiency and access, and curbing corruption.

Under structural adjustment programmes (SAPS), privatization had always been one of the preconditions for loan access from the IFIs and it continues to be the case under the Poverty Reduction Strategy Papers (PRSP) Policy Matrix. Under the PRSP, privatization includes services like water and electricity. There are at least three models of water privatization:

1   The complete sale of public water delivery and treatment systems to private corporations.
2   The granting of long-term leases or concessions allowing corporations to take over delivery of water services and collection of revenues.
3   The granting of contracts for corporations to manage water services for an administration fee.

WATER WARS

Water is undeniably one of the most important natural resources, especially as the world's water becomes more polluted and increasingly out of reach of the poor. The former vice president of the World Bank, Ishmael Serageldi, forecast that the wars of the twenty-first century will be fought over water. True to this prophecy, the first water war was fought in Bolivia after the World Bank refused to renew a US$25 million loan unless water services were privatized. In 2000, the people of Cochabamba ran amok when water rates were increased by a US-based corporation. Similar incidents took place in Lima, Peru, where the rich pay 30 US cents for clean water, while water vendors pay US$3 per cubic foot of unsafe water. It is ironic that in spite of such foresight, and perhaps because of his position as Chair of the Global Water Partnership, Ishmael Serageldi remains one of the prime movers for the privatization of water in developing countries.

In May 2000 Fortune magazine claimed: 'Water promises to be to the twenty-first century what oil was to the twentieth century: the precious commodity that determines the wealth of nations.' The availability or scarcity of water has an impact on virtually every aspect of life and development. As an unsubstitutable resource, local communities have protected water and treated it as a public good that is sacred and beyond commercial value. According to an African saying, water is the only thing one cannot deny even to an enemy. The provision of water needs to be seen as basic and central to human and other forms of life. It should not be regarded as a tradable commodity.

THE WATER DEBATE

In rural areas, debates about water are based on to whom it is seen to belong, to whom it is allocated, and whose rights are violated when it is privatized. As with land and trees, traditional practice values water because of the life it provides and contains. In numerous traditions, bodies of water were known to have spirits that set the rules for water use and extraction of its resources. Water continues to be regarded as a resource that needs to be regulated, not abused or commodified.

Governments and funding partners still focus on increasing private sector participation in rural water provision as one way of ensuring wider coverage. Water projects have been awarded to private contractors in Uganda, for example, in close collaboration with the local District tender boards that had proved themselves incapable of providing the very water services they are now meant to oversee.

Private sector involvement in water entails the construction of physical infrastructure, but not the mobilization of the community to ensure sustainability. Whereas private sector involvement in water management may ensure coverage, availability, quality and efficiency of a service, it certainly eliminates those who cannot afford to pay for water, particularly the women are the principle managers of water provision. Replacing such women with mechanisms put in place by profit makers will not sustain the spiritual and environmental life of water sources, nor ensure continued access and efficient management.

WHO BENEFITS FROM THE PRIVATIZATION OF WATER?

In Tanzania, the Dar es Salaam Water and Sewerage Authority (DAWASA) was asked to privatize water. The Tanzanian government had to raise US$145 million to upgrade DAWASA before it could be privatized. US$47 million of that money was raised from the Africa Development Bank and the rest from the World Bank and the European Investment Bank, and Agence Française de Développement. This effectively increased Tanzania's debt and reduced the chances of the poor to gain access to water and sanitation services.

In Ghana, five multinational corporations bid for Tema Water Service. These corporations are known to have annual sales incomes that are higher than the entire GDP of Ghana. Some of them have questionable social and environmental records. This directly raised concerns about the capacity of the Ghanaian government to monitor, regulate or even hold these companies accountable on social or environmental issues. Once water services are privatized, local governments frequently lack the clout needed to ensure that water quality and pollution standards are met and to penalize corporations who fail to meet them.

The anticipated increase in efficiency of privatized utility companies, when it did occur, in most cases did not result from improved operations. Rather, the ratio of revenue to expenses rose as a result of price increases facilitated by virtual monopoly situations and weak government regulatory mechanisms.

WATER: THE BEST INVESTMENT SECTOR

The market for water and sanitation is increasing globally. It is already a billion dollar industry 40 per cent the size of the oil sector and one third larger than pharmaceuticals. Johan Bastin claims 'water and its infrastructure are the final frontier for private investors to invade'. The big water corporations are also taking advantage of the power and tools of trade and investment in developing countries. They are the true beneficiaries of World Bank and IMF loans and grants.

When Suez, for example, took over water operations in Buenos Aires, all but US$30 million of the US$1 billion required for investment in new infrastructure came from the World Bank, with assistance from the Inter American Development Bank and local Argentine banks. The Polaris Institute (2003) describes how, in March 2001, the World Bank was the major overseas investor (to the tune of US$225 million) in a large water services privatization project in Thailand developed by RWE's subsidiary, Thames Water International.

PRIVATIZATION OF WATER: A CONDITION FOR RENEWAL OF LOANS

A random review reported by the Polaris Institute notes that IMF loans in 40 countries in 2000 revealed that 12 had loan conditions that imposed privatization of water or full cost recovery. This was the case in Tanzania. Nyamugasira and Rowden (2002) observe that while ownership of water supply and sanitation assets in Uganda will remain in the hands of the government, under the World Bank's Poverty Reduction Strategy Credit (PRSC-1) Policy Matrix annex, plans are outlined to privatize the operations of the national water supply and sanitation services in the urban centres and have the service provided via management contracts with local and international private operators.

During the Poverty Eradication Action Plan (PEAP) that gave birth to the Uganda PRSP, civil society clearly did not call for the privatization of water utilities to international investors. Nevertheless the process of privatizing water is underway, with plans to have end-use paying customers finance improvements before the utility can be sold to the foreign investor. Privatization of water in Uganda, therefore, will only take place once consumers have shouldered the burden of ensuring that the system is financed so that it is profitable even before it is sold. These 'reforms' also ensure that the cross-subsidies that had been built into the price tariff structure are unbundled. This means that there will be no provision in the privatized water system for positively discriminating in favour of poor water consumers by ensuring wealthier consumers subsidize them.

The involvement of IFIs in financing private water corporations and using privatization as a condition for accessing loans is not only unjust; it is also an imposition that interferes with national decision making and in some instances disregards civil society's concerns and priorities. In addition, it pressurizes governments to be more accountable to IFIs than they are to their citizens.

If gender and civil society are disregarded in water management, governments will be unable to resist a global industry of vast corporations such as Vivendi

Universal and Suez, popularly called the General Motors and Ford of the global water industry.

References

Bond, Patrick, David McDonald and Gregg Ruiters (2001). 'Water Privatization in SADC: The State of the Debate.' Municipal Service Project, October.

DFID and UNDP (2002). 'Linking Poverty Reduction and Environmental Management: Policy Challenges and Opportunities', January.

Madava, Tinaishe (2000). South African News Features: South African Research and Documentation Centres (SARDC). Harare, Zimbabwe.

Nyamugasira, Warren and Rick Rowden (2002). 'New Strategies, Old Conditions: Do the New IMF and World Bank Loans Support Country's Poverty Reduction Goals?' Kampala and Washington, DC, April.

Polaris Institute (2003). Global Water Grab: How Corporations are Planning to Take Control of Local Water Services.' Ottawa, January.

Retallack, Simon (1997). Eclogist, Vol. 27, No. 4 (July/August).

Shiva, Vandana (2000). Third World Network Features, Malaysia.

Ssentamu, Dumba (2000). 'The Impact of Privatization on Social Services.' SAPRI, Uganda NGO Forum, June.

11

Conclusions

Athena Peralta

OVERVIEW

The September 2003 internal encounter organized by the World Council of
Churches (WCC) on the policies of the International Monetary Fund (IMF) and
World Bank had the following objectives:

- To elaborate on a common vision and coherent strategies within the ecumenical movement to address the policies implemented by the IMF and
  World Bank.
- To enable representatives from churches, agencies and partners from
  social movements to search for consistent and effective ways to promote
  ecumenical responses to the policies of the IMF and World Bank from the
  perspective of people in poverty.
- To discuss the issues that had to be raised with the IMF and World Bank
  at the second external encounter in October 2003.

This chapter affirms the spiritual, moral and ethical basis for churches' engagement with the IMF and the World Bank, points out the challenges churches face
in this process and highlights the main issues.

GROUNDS FOR EXTERNAL ENCOUNTER

The WCC had been invited by the IMF and World Bank to enter into dialogue.
Just as Jesus engaged with different personalities and authorities in his time, we,
as churches and Christians, are open to constructive encounters and a genuine
exchange of views with the IMF and World Bank. We bring into these external
encounters a rich diversity of experiences and forms of witness. The WCC and the
broader ecumenical movement represent a global network that can contribute
from specific experiences at local levels in many parts of the world. This strength
of the global ecumenical movement constitutes an important building block in
external encounters with powerful global institutions.

Testimonies and research findings from our sisters and brothers in Africa, Asia
and Latin America show that the harsh economic measures imposed by the IMF
and World Bank as 'conditionalities' for providing loans, debt relief and bail-outs
in times of crises, as well as the unremitting flow of payments for debts often
incurred by governments under illegitimate conditions, have a devastating impact
on basic human rights and the chances of survival of millions of impoverished and
vulnerable people. In our external encounters with the IMF and World Bank, we
must lift up the voices – the 'cries for life' – of these people, for whom God has
expressed a preferential option. The point of departure in these external encounters should be the loving message of Jesus: that all should have life in all its fullness, here and now, and in the future.

As churches and Christians, we are called to give witness of the hope that is in us. This hope is the basis for our passion for the possible. Our rich ecumenical heritage – of studies as well as specific projects – indicates viable alternatives to unjust and unsustainable systems and policies, both globally and locally.[1] Thus, the claim 'there is no alternative' has to be rejected.

The spirituality of life, which is basic to our Christian faith, is intrinsically at odds with prevailing political–economic arrangements and policies that create and exacerbate human suffering. Therefore, we believe that, eventually, nothing less than a fundamental shift in political–economic paradigms is necessary if humankind is to become an instrument of God in striving for the vision of just, participatory and sustainable communities.

In summary, as the WCC publication Lead Us Not Into Temptation points out, we, as churches and Christians, are called to:

- prophetically criticize injustices and create new visions;
- courageously resist political and economic powers;
- advocate for reforms and fundamental changes so that political and economic structures serve life;
- live out the alternatives of God's kingdom.

CHALLENGES ON THE ROAD

In external encounters with the IMF and World Bank we face several challenges:

1. There is considerable confusion about language and concepts:
   - We look at the same things, but see different things.
   - We use the same concepts and terms, but our meanings are different.
   - We listen to the same words, but hear different things.

In external encounters, greater clarity and transparency are needed in the use of concepts and how they are operationalized.

2. No unwarranted legitimacy should be given to policies of global institutions which run counter to our basic convictions. This requires an open, straightforward attitude from us, as well as from the IMF and World Bank.

3. Participants should assess carefully which 'arenas' for discussion (global, regional, national, local) are the most useful and appropriate for obtaining the desired results and objectives of dialogue.

4. Participants should guard against claiming absolute moral, spiritual or technical authority and rejecting other views and convictions as unrealistic or ethically indefensible.

5. A convincing challenge to the IMF and World Bank must be complemented with internal appeals for consistency in terms of levels and styles of consumption and production within our churches.

ISSUES FOR THE SECOND WCC–IMF–WORLD BANK ENCOUNTER

The first WCC–IMF–World Bank encounter in February 2003 identified a number of issues to be raised in the next encounter:

- Participation of civil society in development. The issue of people's participation in development policy-making, implementation, monitoring and evaluation will be looked at in terms of roles and processes, with emphasis on the external debt problem and the Poverty Reduction Strategy Papers (PRSP) approach of the IMF and World Bank.

- Institutional governance and accountability. The need for more democratic and representative governance of international institutions such as the IMF and World Bank and accountability for their development policies and actions.
- Respective roles of public and private sectors in development. Roles/responsibilities and the interplay of states and markets in development policy and poverty eradication efforts will be explored. Dealing with governments lacking in legitimacy will also be tackled.
- Challenges of globalization. The following questions will be addressed, among others: What are the dynamics of the globalization process? Who are the key actors? What are the impacts in terms of growth and equity?

The internal encounter affirms the need for a critical exchange with the IMF and World Bank on the issues outlined above. Concern over privatization should be discussed under 'respective roles of public and private sectors in development' and possible and viable alternatives be added under 'challenges of globalization'.

As regards 'institutional governance and accountability', during the first encounter the IMF and the World Bank recognized the dominant position of the rich countries ('shareholders') in their institutions. This seriously compromises the democratic nature of these institutions.

We recommend the inclusion of two additional issues for discussion:

- Responsibility. Who takes responsibility for grave mistakes made by major actors such as the IMF and World Bank (e.g. odious debts)?
- Conditionality. The conditionalities used by the IMF and World Bank reflect prevailing political–economic power relations and ideologies, contrary to the stated objectives of their policies as outlined in the PRSP framework.

WORKING TOGETHER FOR JUST, PARTICIPATORY AND SUSTAINABLE GLOBAL SYSTEMS

The internal encounter yielded inspiring material not only for WCC-IMF-World Bank encounters, but also for the varied ecumenical initiatives on economic justice, such as ongoing debt cancellation campaigns in adherence to the Jubilee tradition and the 'Trade for Peoples' campaign. We bring these fruits with us in our continuing work towards the building of just, participatory and sustainable global systems that serve life for all.

Note

1   See, for example, the work of the WCC and the ecumenical movement on the issue of ecological sustainability and the concept of just, participatory and sustainable societies, as well as the operationalization of this concept through global networks of local actors (report of the Advisory Group on Economic Matters, The International Financial System: An Ecumenical Critique, WCC, Geneva, 1985), and the work of the Ecumenical Church Loan Fund (ECLOF) and Oikocredit.

Appendix A

Meditation for Opening Worship

Seong-Won Park

REMOVE YOUR SANDALS FROM YOUR FEET! EXODUS 3:1-15

When we apply for a job, we are usually asked by the employer to submit a curriculum vitae. As we all know very well, the curriculum vitae is a personal history, a history which explains when and where the person was born, what kind of education the person has received, and what kind of personal experiences and jobs the person has had. The word curriculum comes from the Latin word curro, which means 'run' or 'flow' in English. Many other interesting words are derived from curro, such as 'current', meaning a course of movement, a tendency or passing onward.

One descriptive meaning of the word current is in fact 'a continuous flow of something like water or air'. The economy should be like a flow of water, flowing from the upper level to the lower level. The economic word currency also comes from the Latin word curro. In this word, we encounter the same image, the image of water flowing. Currency or money should keep flowing or running without staying in any one place. It should continue to flow, not accumulate in the hands of the few, but reach every corner and people of society.

Calvin emphasized that money should move so that many can benefit. Money is moving actively today, maybe more actively than ever before. The problem is that is not moving for the benefit of all, but only for a few people. Money flows backward, not from the rich to the poor as Calvin suggested, but from the poor to the rich. If water flows backward, it is abnormal. Today's movement of currency is abnormal. If that is so, it needs to be corrected.

Let me come back to the curriculum vitae. We Asians also have a particular word for curriculum vitae. The Chinese word for curriculum vitae is Yee Ryuck Seo (in Korean pronunciation). Seo means 'writing' or 'record', Ryuck means 'history' and Yee means 'shoe' or 'sandals'. Therefore, the Chinese word for curriculum vitae, Yee Ryuck Seo, means 'a record of history of a person's shoe prints'. I don't know whether the phrase 'shoe prints' is possible, but maybe we could identify it with footprints. A curriculum vitae is a record of history which shows how a person has left their footprints in their life, meaning how one has lived one's life.

When Moses responded to God's calling, God asked him to remove the sandals from his feet, for the place on which Moses stood was holy ground. What does this mean? God's request came to Moses when he was about to be given a divine mission to liberate the Hebrew slaves from Egyptian bondage. In a sense, Moses was already engaged in a liberation movement when he killed an Egyptian who had been beating one of his kinsfolk. In a sense, that was a liberation movement initiated by humans. He even adopted violent means.

However, in the Midian wilderness he receives a new mandate for the liberation of his people. And he is asked by God to remove his sandals, because the place on which he is standing is holy ground. What is the relationship between receiving a new mission and removing sandals? It could be understood as the message that a divinely inspired liberation movement must replace a human initiative.

By removing sandals from human feet, we come to rely on a divine principle for liberation. By the removing of sandals, we hear attentively God's way of liberation. As Isaiah 55:8 has said, God's thoughts are not our thoughts; nor are our ways God's ways. By removing the sandals from our feet, we commit ourselves to follow God's way of liberation, not the human way.

Today, there are many arrogant claims that human beings can achieve human liberation. Neoliberal global capitalism suggests unlimited economic growth can liberate human beings from all kinds of problems, like poverty, disease and even social conflict. Technological developments and economic growth can continue without limit until all the problems of human communities are solved.

Francis Fukuyama, one of the leading figures in the neoliberal school, said that even human beings of a violent nature can be cured by neuropharmacological developments and medicines such as Retalin and Prozac. When you become nervous, violent or militant, you can take a pill to calm yourself and become peaceful. If this kind of neuropharmacological development is ever achieved, there might be no need for the church to exist. We will not need to work on the Decade to Overcome Violence. The most effective way will be to provide Retalin and Prozac to calm the violent nature of humanity. Isn't this a comedy?

I was shocked to listen to a Canadian medical scientist who advocated human cloning: 'We are now entering into the divine area', he said on CNN television. This is the doctrinal faith of the neoliberals. The neo-conservatives in the White House seek to convince the whole world that they can liberate Iraq and punish the axis of evil using their empire's forces, believing that those forces are unprecedented in their might. As the Palmist said, the One who sits in heaven laughs at this arrogant attitude (Psalm 2:4).

Today, the time has come for human beings to remove the sandals from their feet. The shoe prints that human history has been making turn out to be a mistake. Human history – humanity's curriculum vitae – has always taken a zigzag path. We need to challenge the World Bank, the IMF and the current empire to remove their sandals and receive a new mandate from God for authentic poverty eradication and authentic liberation.

Appendix B

Meditation for Opening Worship

Aruna Gnanadason

ALL ARE INVITED TO THE FIESTA OF GOD! LUKE 9:10–17
A while ago, I had the privilege of worshipping with a small Aymara Lutheran community high in the Andes mountains in Bolivia. After worship we were invited to participate in a community lunch with that poor congregation. I saw no cooking, no hustle and bustle of women running around busily (as it would have been on a similar occasion in India), and no smoke from any chimneys. Being a bit hungry, I wondered where our lunch was! Suddenly, I saw a long piece of cloth being placed on the ground in front of the church. The community of women, children and men sat down in an orderly fashion on either side of the cloth and we were invited to join them. The women unloosened the shawls wrapped around their waists and poured onto the cloth many kinds of potatoes. After a prayer of thanks for the food, we had a meal of potatoes. As we were special guests, a woman near us opened another piece of cloth and gave us pieces of delicious home made cheese.

We ate our fill and I wondered what would happen to the remaining potatoes – of which there were plenty. After a quiet signal from the elder, everyone took a share, again in an orderly way. Everyone, even those who had brought no food with them, took a share of the potatoes – it was done in such a matter of fact way, almost as if it was the natural thing to do. It was indeed a fiesta of God to which all there were invited. I hasten to add that this was no exotic or one-off event: we were told that all congregations do the same thing every Sunday.

It was a moving experience – paradigmatic of the story from the Bible of the five loaves and two fishes. It was this miracle story of the multiplication of the loaves and fishes that came to my mind as I saw the potatoes tumble onto the cloth from the folds of the skirts of the Aymara women – an amazing story of the grace, generosity and hospitality of the poor.

I first heard the story of the five loaves and two fishes as a child. Jesus' miraculous power multiplied the loaves and fishes so that they could serve 5,000 men. If to this number we add women and children – in those times, they were not counted –it is even more miraculous. I also remember when I first heard another interpretation of this text. It was in a meeting of the Student Christian Movement (the national part of the WSCF) when I was at university. Dr K. C. Abraham, the Indian liberation theologian, retold the story for us. He told it to us indeed as a story of the miraculous power of Jesus, but a miracle with a difference – it was a miracle of sharing and of caring for each other. Seeing the contribution of the five loaves and two fishes from the young boy, the community took out the food each of them had carried, perhaps wrapped in their shawls, and a fiesta was prepared!

The disciples were surprised when Jesus so carelessly asked them to feed all the people – their first reaction is to ask Jesus to send the people home so that they could fend for themselves. Then they turn to the market – that seems the only solution. I detect a note of sarcasm in their voices when they suggest that perhaps Jesus is asking them to go out at the last minute and buy food for 5,000 persons. To them, the people are just a nuisance! Perhaps they thought that an act of charity might make the problem go away – Jesus and the people would leave them alone! Perhaps a poverty reduction strategy would help, or a technological fix – anything but having to listen to the people, encouraging them to change their own condition, encouraging them to discover from within their own resources their own solutions.

Jesus asks them to take an alternative path – he turns the situation into an opportunity for the people who are gathered. He ensures that all are fed from among their own resources. Those who had more would have had to have given more so that all could be fed, just as it was among the Aymara community. Jesus encourages the community to reclaim what is rightfully theirs. He does not depend on the market!

Jesus gives them more than food; he teaches them the art of sharing. He teaches them how to be a community of love: this is implied by that way he asks them to sit down in groups – those who had some food with them and those who did not had to sit together. The gospel writer tells us that Jesus then took the bread and blessed it, broke it and gave it to the disciples to distribute to the people. It is amazing that in the midst of a simple event of sharing food, the author uses this sacramental language – well before the actual Christ-event is recorded. This act of Christ gives new meaning and significance to sharing in the body and blood of Christ. Today, in the context of an unjust and unequal world, in a world of continuing unacceptable hunger, the sacraments symbolize a strong word of hope – an alternative fiesta of God. And on the other side of the coin there are the grotesque levels of wealth. Here, the sacraments symbolize the gift of radical sharing – and . not just a sharing of the surplus we have after all (or more than all) our needs are met. And not just charitable acts either.

The Bible tells us that after all were fed there are 12 baskets of leftovers. It is interesting how often the Bible includes these small details. Perhaps like the Aymara community, this surplus of 12 baskets was shared by all, so that even those who brought no food with them could go home with something. I stretch my imagination further and imagine that this would perhaps feed a family for another day. All who are willing to share are welcome to the fiesta of God. Those who have more can share more – so that all can be fed. And yet the Aymara community made me realize that it is those who have little who are the most generous. I am sure you have all experienced similar surprising acts of welcome and hospitality in poor homes.

Sisters and brothers, I hope this image will accompany us as we continue to reflect on the challenges we need to take with us in our encounter with power and arrogant might in the form of the World Bank and IMF. Will they be willing to share their loaves and fishes, or will they send the people away with small concessions for which the poor are expected to be grateful? We have already seen that this is not easy. All the resources we bring to the table from our ecumenical history – from our uncompromising commitment to justice and all the marvellous resources that lie embedded in our own faith heritage, including the basic understanding of God's option for the poor – seem to be put to the test. But I believe that we in the ecumenical movement, we as Christians, really have no choice: we are challenged to spread with courage and foolish hope the gospel promise that all the 'little ones' in the world – right down to the poorest of the poor – are welcome at the fiesta of God.

Appendix C
Bible Study

Priscilla Singh

TALKING TO THE POWERFUL: 1 SAMUEL 25:1–31
I have decided to draw on a woman's story. You cannot expect a woman from the
South, like me, who is working with and for women, to do anything else but
choose a woman as a role model. Therefore, I have chosen a text that focuses on
a woman who gathered her resource and her wits about her to confront power in
what was a very volatile situation.

It was certainly no ordinary occasion, but a sheep shearing festival, where usually there is open house, much rejoicing and an abundance of food for everyone.
There are three sets of people in this story:

1   David, who was shepherding sheep, had been anointed by the prophet
        Samuel to take over from Saul as king of Israel when the time was right.
        Because of his prowess and increasing popularity with the masses, he
        earns the wrath of Saul, who is now seeking to kill him after the death of
        Samuel. David had to take refuge in the wilderness with his 600 follow-
        ers and as leader is obligated to feed them and keep up their morale.
        However, he has already misused his military might in order to take sheep
        from the shepherds of Nabal. Running for his life, living in desperate con-
        ditions with desperate men, David thinks it is justifiable to seek for food
        from the rich man of the locality whose flock he and his men had helped
        protect, especially when it is a festive occasion. The lesson this group
        gives us is that people, however poor, have much to offer and are willing
        to share what they have. They should not be discounted simply because
        they have no economic power.
2   Nabal is not only very rich, he is also well connected, because he is one
        of the descendents of Caleb. His wealth and connections makes him arro-
        gant. He thinks he can neglect and insult others, and not heed their advice.
        He is quite brutal and direct to the messengers from David calling David
        a more or less a servant who had deserted his master and simply chooses
        not to think about the consequences of his words. This is the myth that the
        powerful shroud themselves with; they are so powerful that they can
        deign to be arrogant, override anybody's need or well placed advice and
        can get away with their ways. Economic power is no insulation against
        aggression as September 11 reminds us. I am not sure whether this is the
        case yet with the organizations because they are now taking the pain to
        dialogue with us despite our ideological divide. This gives us two possi-
        bilities. Learning each others' vocabulary and concepts to either outsmart
        one another or on a more hopeful note, listen, share and learn from one
        another so that we follow a life centered ethics and not life negating poli-
        cies.

3   Abigail was a woman of those times who is supposed to be only known as someone's wife. She dares to defy one her husband and confront the other. The normal reaction of a woman in such a critical situation when a bunch of 400 guys are coming to take revenge could only be in the following ways. Go and put some sense into the husband who is bringing such a calamity on them and ask him to apologize and make amends. But Abigail that knew his riches had made him arrogant and like the servants testify 'he does not listen to anyone'. So she did not follow this futile course of action. The second is to simply cut and run. She could have taken some wealth and some servants and put a lot of distance between the men and herself and allow these warring men to sort things out! She did not do that because personal preservation was the last in her agenda. The last option is to be fatalistic and say 'Que. Sara Sara' like some of the world is tending to say when they think that they cannot resist the impact of economic globalization!

What resources can we draw from this ancient story to inform us today?
We develop a sense the rightness of things. There were no treaties signed or accords made between Nabal and David to make David's claim for food valid except an ethical sense. He did a good turn by protecting the sheep day and night without getting anything in return and so he deserves some food at least at the festival time as a token of appreciation. Caleb can turn around and say but we did not sign any agreement about this! He might be right if we go by written agreements. But the laws are written in human hearts as the Scripture informs us and not left just in books and papers to define how we reciprocate. So we are not tripping about TRIPPS here but what the churches together with the NGOs are all the time calling out to the financial institutions, 'please care for life for all and not only for the rich and the powerful, that it is in ensuring the safety and security of all in their own countries that the safety of the rest of the world rests upon. I marvel at the audacity of some to claim intellectual property rights as though they got all these on their own. Every Good gifts come from above the creator and we are only stewards. If God has put a right on God's creation where we would all be. The most precious things we need for our survival; the air, the water and the food that grow are made free by God.

We have an ear to the ground: Abigail listened to the advice of the grass root people the ones who live close to the reality and really feel the pinch. When people like Stanley and Helen and others who relate the global to the local we better listen because you know what you are talking about. You are the early warning system that we have to listen to and make the needed connections.

We keep a discerning heart to study what is happening around us and to foresee the outcome. Abigail smelt disaster, knowing her husband and David's background. But she also understands that the conflict came because of hunger and she immediately prepares to rectify that need, first by taking enough food to the hungry men. We give people what they need before we talk of treaties and consensus.

Courage to defy and ignore if the powerful who will not listen but try to negotiate and appeal to the sensibilities of the willing to renegotiate.

Power of suggestion: There is tremendous power in suggestion. In an experiment with a group of students, the students were told that scientists have proved that brown-eyed children were smarter than the blue eyed ones. Immediately the brown eyed students started doing well in class. After some time the students were told that they had been misinformed and that it is the blue eyed ones who were the smarter ones and the situation changed for the blue eyed! Perhaps we still need to entertain some hope and appeal to the goodness of the organizations. William Sloane Coffin Jr. says 'Hope arouses, as nothing else can arouse, a passion for the possible". A word of encouragement can make the difference between giving up and going on' and that we need to offer to those who are actively involved. The WTO is under tremendous pressure to perform which is why its Director General has come out with the following statement yesterday at the opening in Cancún. 'We face a choice here in Cancún. Either we continue to strengthen the multilateral trading system and the world economy or we flounder and we add to the prevailing uncertainties. 'The eyes of the world are on this conference and people will judge us by the choice we make. 'There is only one possible answer. We have to deliver on the first choice,' he said. So we need to persist and keep the heat on.

Just to wrap up Abigail took the risk and broke the myth that power is in the hands of the rich and the mighty

- By acquiring the power to perceive and assess the situation
- Having a thorough background knowledge of the powerful actors at play
- By consulting and giving power to the grass roots to define and name the situation
- Identifying the root cause of injustice
- Responding to the immediate need of appeasing the hunger of the many
- Dialoguing to clear the ground of suspicion and hurt
- Diplomatically reminding the high calling of the person who was out to kill and by appealing to the goodness of the man reminding him of his high calling.
- Igniting hope in a seemingly impossible situation through words of encouragement

What parallels can we see in this story to suit our situation?
The one who has the potential power to do enormous good can be likened to Nabal if they do not care to listen or care to share a little of their wealth. They forget that their wealth is created by the sweat of others who willingly work for them and make them rich and therefore their loyalty should be with the workers. Abigail did not pay attention to such a person. And that perhaps is what we may have to do in the end as our course of action if the financial institutions persistently close their ears to our cries. And if they do that then they may have to as well die like Nabal. Because in the end that want happens to him.

The desperately poor can be likened to the group of men in the wilderness headed by David who want some one to do act on their behalf. You leave them without meeting their needs then, we will have a dangerous situation in our hands before long and we cannot then entirely blame them for atrocities or brand them as trouble makers. The poor and needy have only these options, to cry out for help, or submit to slow death in indignity or commit suicide in utter despair. We need to open up options for them to live and to live well.

The mediators, the NGOs, the intellectuals could be likened to Abigail and the servants who want to save the situation and protect lives that are endangered. Contrary to the popular belief that it is by might or by economic power a situation is changed from potentially dangerous to peaceable one, we see in this story the power of persuasion of a woman presumed in those days to be the utmost powerless. It is again a myth that the marginalized are powerless and that power is in the hand of the rich and the mighty. Power is in the hands of those who collude to save lives and side with the needy giving them hope for a better future.

What is power?
Power is not what we have or what we acquire by virtue of birth, occupation or right connection but as the one that comes from God and rises from within. One of the translation of the Lord's Prayer from Aramaic clearly specifies this 'From you is born all ruling will, the power and the life to do'

The German words Macht (power) and mögen (to want, to like) are derived from the Old High German root magan. Bishop Bärbel Von Wartenberg- Potter concludes that at least in German, 'Power and liking, power and love are somehow related to one another and that the origin of these words still show us something of how people are enabled, empowered through love; love of people and the love of God. Whenever the connection between power and love is lost, or the one is no longer bound up with the other, power becomes something menacing and dangerous, it degenerates into domination and arbitrariness. ....it creates distance between those who have power and those who have not. It surrounds itself with status symbols. It seeks to increase its means of control (knowledge, authority, money) rather than sharing them. Can we possibly break this dynamic of wielding power?'[1]

It may be interesting to note that when the Prophet Isaiah spells out doom in chapter 10:1-3, he begins by saying 'Woe to those who make unjust laws, to those who issue oppressive decrees, to deprive the poor of their rights and withhold justice from the oppressed of my people' So it is not only the life you live in your private domain that is going to cause us woe, but our colluding either through ignorance, apathy or silence in creating and perpetuating unjust laws that are primarily going to get us into trouble!

We are powerful people too and it is a tight rope walking between rendering service and exercising power. Only by staying closer to the forces that can correct us, and protect us from the love of power that we can achieve the right balance.

Here is one such collective force of women who wrote the Declaration of the Women's Global Strategies Meeting:

> We are the women who hunger – for rice, home, freedom, each other ourselves.
>
> We are the women, who thirst – for clean water and laughter literacy and love.
>
> We have existed at all times, in every society. We have survived femicide.
> We have rebelled and left clues.

We are continuity, weaving future from past, logic with lyric.
We are women who wear broken bones, voices, minds, hearts – but we are women who dare whisper NO.
We are women whose souls no fundamentalist cage can contain.
We are women who refuse to permit the sowing of death in our gardens, air, rivers, seas.
We are each precious, unique, necessary. We are strengthened and blessed and relieved at not having to be all the same. We are the daughters of longing. We are the mothers in labor to birth the politics of the 21st century.
We are the women men warned us about.
We are the women who know that all issues are ours, who will reclaim our wisdom, reinvent our tomorrow, question and redefine everything, including power.
We have worked now for decades to name the details of our need, rage, hope, and vision. We have broken our silence, exhausted our patience. We are weary of listing on our suffering – to entertain or be simply ignored. We are done with vague words and real waiting; famishing for action, dignity, joy. We intend to do more than merely endure and survive.
They have tried to deny us, define us, denounce us: to jail, enslave, gas, rape, beat, burn bury and bore us. Yet nothing not even the offer to save their failed system can grasp us.
For thousands of years, women have had responsibility without power – while men have had power without responsibility. We offer those men who risk being brothers, a balance future, a hand. But with or without them we will go on.
For we are the old ones, the new breed, the natives who came first and lasted, indigenous to an utterly different dimension. We are the girl child in Zambia, grandmother in Burma, the woman in El Salvador and Afghanistan, Finland and Fiji……………All this we are. We are intensity, energy, the people speaking, who no longer will wait and who cannot be stopped."[2]

Yes individually these simple women can be discounted as people with limited power, but together, they are a force to reckon with. I often use this quote from a stubborn old man of the recent past who struggled with the mighty empire of his time to create the biggest democracy. Gandhi. He said ' A small body of determined spirits fired by an unquenchable faith in their mission can alter the course of history' I strongly feel that this small gathering could be such a one. May God help us to be so.

Notes

1   "We will not Hang Our Harps on the Willows - Global Sisterhood and God's Song" by Bärbel Von Wartenberg- Potter, published by The Cross Road Publishing Company, , New York, 1987, p 61

2   The Alternative Forum, Issue No7, Special edition 2001, p12.

Appendix D

PARTICIPANTS

Christer Akesson, Church of Sweden
Lawrence Brew, World Student Christian Federation
Baffour Dokyi Amoa, Fellowship of Christian Councils and Churches in West Africa (FECCIWA)
Pamela Brubaker, California Lutheran University
Clarissa Balan, World YWCA
Karen Bloomquist, Lutheran World Federation
Sharon Bradshaw, Caribbean Conference of Churches
Franklin Canelos, Latin American Council of Churches
Ulrich Duchrow, Kairos Europa
Obispo Aldo M. Etchegoyen, Evangelical Methodist Church of Argentina
Elizabeth Ferris, World Council of Churches
Aruna Gnanadason, World Council of Churches
Bob Goudzwaard
Carlos Ham, World Council of Churches
Michiel Hardon, World Council of Churches
Eberhard Hitzler, Protestant Church in Germany
Guillermo Kerber, World Council of Churches
Freddy Knutsen, World Council of Churches
Samuel Kobia, World Council of Churches
Kwame Labi, World Council of Churches
Peter Lanzet, Evangelischer Entwicklungsdienst e.V. EED
Flemming Larsen, International Monetary Fund
Georges Lemopoulos, World Council of Churches
Erik Lysén, Church of Sweden Aid
Deenabandhu Manchala, World Council of Churches
William Mansour, Middle East Council of Churches
Katherine Marshall, World Bank
Dinis Matsolo, Christian Council of Mozambique
Juan Michel, World Council of Churches
Alois Moeller, Bread for the World
Ulrich Moeller, EKD-Evangelical Church of Westphalia
Rogate Mshana, World Council of Churches
Jennifer Müller, World Student Christian Federation
Alicia Nebot, Latin American Council of Churches
Seong-Won Park, World Alliance of Reformed Churches
Edouard Paultre, Protestant Federation of Haiti
Peter Pavlovic, Conference of European Churches
Athena Peralta, World Council of Churches
Konrad Raiser, World Council of Churches
Samuel Rizk, Middle East Council of Churches

Martin Robra, World Council of Churches
Ioan Sauca, World Council of Churches
Gabriel M. P. Sharma, Pacific Conference of Churches
Pavel Shashkin, Moscow Patriarchate
Priscilla Singh, Lutheran World Federation
Peter Söderbaum, Mälardalen University
Atle Sommerfeldt, Norwegian Church Aid
Christoph Stückelberger, Bread for All
Elisabeth S. Tapia, World Council of Churches
Michael H. Taylor, University of Birmingham
Molefe Tsele, South African Council of Churches
Robert W. F. van Drimmelen, APRODEV
Gertraud Maria Wachmann, Focolare Movement – Economy of Communion in Switzerland
Hellen Grace Akwii Wangusa, Anglican Church, rep. AWEPON and AACC
Tony Waworuntu, Christian Conference of Asia
Josef P. Widyatmadja, Christian Conference of Asia
Stanley William, United Evangelical Church in India
Margarita E. Witte-Rang, Oiko Credit
Lian Xiao, Chinese Academy of Social Sciences

Observers
Alexei E. Bodrov, St. Andrews Biblical Theological College
Lene Fretheim, World Alliance of YMCAs
Agustinus Kermite, Social Welfare Guidance Foundation, Indonesia
Anna Marsiana, Social Welfare Guidance Foundation, Indonesia
Marius Müller, Focolare Movement – Economy of Communion in Switzerland
Clara Squarzon, Focolare Movement – Economy of Communion in Switzerland
Ignacio Trujillo, World Council of Churches (steward)
Alexandre Veyrat-Pontet, World Student Christian Federation
Daniel Wieser, World Council of Churches

L'impression et le façonnage ont été réalisés
à l'Imprimerie LUSSAUD - 85200 Fontenay-le-Comte

Dépôt légal 2ᵉ trimestre 2004 - n° 3740 – N° d'impression : 203520